# HE LIFTS MY HEAD HIGH

# HE LIFTS MY HEAD HIGH

3-Minute
**Daily Affirmations**
for Christians

**Jaseña S'vani**

ALTHEA
PRESS

Interior and Cover Designer: Peatra Jariya
Art Producer: Karen Beard
Production Manager: Oriana Siska
Editor: Rachel Feldman
Production Editor: Melissa Edeburn
Illustration © sanchenet1 / iStock, cover
Author photo courtesy of D. Divine Photography

ISBN: Print 978-1-64152-501-5 | eBook 978-1-64152-502-2

# Contents

Therefore whoever hears these sayings of Mine, and does them, I will liken him to a wise man who built his house on the rock: and the rain descended, the floods came, and the winds blew and beat on that house; and it did not fall, for it was founded on the rock.

# Introduction

**GROWING UP, I TOTALLY MISUNDERSTOOD GOD.**

You would think that a preacher's kid, of all people, would be totally spirited in their faith, but I just wasn't. Even though I lived in the church the majority of the week, my mind was elsewhere. I knew who this "God" guy was, but I thought of Him as a distant higher power—floating around in Heaven, managing the world around me—even letting bad things happen. God was unattainable in my eyes, so I distanced myself from Him.

It wasn't until I had an opportunity to experience God in a language that I understood that I truly met the God of the universe. As an avid athlete, I signed up to compete in a 20-hour sports marathon. A quarter of the way through, my body was getting very weak—it was failing me. I remember my knees giving out and feeling like my body was breaking down. It was as if all the burdens and pressures of my life had finally caught up to me. In that moment, as a dear friend of mine prayed for me, I experienced what it means to die to yourself in order to come alive in spirit. I slowed down, looked up, and felt everything give way. It was as though God had peeled the pain off my heart, the negativity from my mind, and the fear from my soul. I looked straight ahead and finished the competition stronger than I had started. I gave my life to Christ that night.

Why am I telling you this? Because, as Christians, we must learn to let go of our earthly ways of thinking (die to ourselves) and use the Word of God to maneuver through the world (take up the cross). The burdens of life are weights that we need to shake off daily, and the affirmations in this book are intended to help you on that journey. There's an affirmation for every day of the year, with each month starting with a longer devotion. You'll be inspired, challenged, and refreshed through scripture, hymns, and other great quotes. The best part about this book is that even when you finish the devotions, you can reuse it for years to come. Or better yet—pass it on to someone else who needs it.

Wherever you are in your life, God's Word is going to inspire you to live more freely than ever before by surrendering to His love. I'm praying that as you journey through this book, His scripture will come alive in a new, creative way for you.

## READY TO GET INSPIRED?

# 1

# Foundation in Christ

> But blessed are those who trust in the LORD and
> have made the LORD their hope and confidence.
> They are like trees planted along a riverbank,
> with roots that reach deep into the water.

**JEREMIAH 17:7-8 NLT**

Jeremiah was appointed by God to warn His people, the people of Jerusalem, that they were headed toward destruction. God's people loved and worshiped the Lord, but as time progressed, they turned their hearts away from Him and began to worship idols. Does this sound familiar? Sometimes we get so distracted by superficial goals that we lose sight of what's important. And sometimes even when we're pursuing worthwhile goals, laziness gets the better of us.

In this verse, Jeremiah is reminding us to stay rooted in Christ. Never forget the principles that got you to where you are in life today. When we stay rooted in that foundation, we will stay prosperous, and most importantly—we will stay close to God!

2

Fight the good fight of faith, lay hold on eternal life,
to which you were also called and have confessed the
good confession in the presence of many witnesses.

1 TIMOTHY 6:12 NKJV

A new year means new beginnings, new choices to
be made, and new opportunities to build the life you
desire. Remember that your ability to prosper this year
is charged with the same power that was unleashed by
your confession of faith.

3

Another year of mercies, of faithfulness and grace;
Another year of gladness in the shining of Thy face;
Another year of leaning upon Thy loving breast;
Another year of trusting, of quiet, happy rest.

"ANOTHER YEAR IS DAWNING"
BY FRANCES RIDLEY HAVERGAL

A new year offers fresh opportunities for God to show
you more of Himself. Prioritize getting to know God on
a deeper level this year.

But You, O LORD, are a shield for me,
my glory and the One who lifts up my head.

PSALM 3:3 NKJV

As you tackle your to-do list today, know that God is
protecting every step you take. Lean on the One who
loves you, and know that with Him anything is possible.

I've learned that people will forget what you said,
people will forget what you did, but people will
never forget how you made them feel.

MAYA ANGELOU

Practice Christ's love and be vigilant in your actions
toward others today. Your treatment of someone
could change the trajectory of his or her life in
unexpected ways.

# 6

But those who wait on the LORD
shall renew their strength; they shall mount up
with wings like eagles, they shall run and not
be weary, they shall walk and not faint.

ISAIAH 40:31 NKJV

Aim to find joy in the journey today and view life's struggles through a lens of love and grace. Trust in the Lord; with Him by your side, you can make it through anything.

# 7

He redeems me from death and crowns
me with love and tender mercies.

PSALM 103:4 NLT

To trust means to love, and to love means to abandon all exit strategies. God will NEVER leave you. Let His perfect love satisfy your soul!

If you can't fly, then run; if you can't run,
then walk; if you can't walk, then crawl. But whatever
you do, you have to keep moving forward.

MARTIN LUTHER KING JR.

No matter where He has placed you in life today, God
has given you exactly what you need to be success-
ful. Ask Him to show you the tools He's given you, and
always remember that the greatest tool of all is love!

Therefore humble yourselves
under the mighty hand of God,
that He may exalt you in due time,
casting all your care upon Him,
for He cares for you.

1 PETER 5:6-7 NKJV

In a world that values confidence and strength above
all else, remember that humility is even more important.
You will be stronger than ever if you remember that your
accomplishments come from God.

# 10

Happiness is when what you think, what you
say, and what you do are in harmony.

MAHATMA GANDHI

Too often we are fooled into believing that happiness is
found in our tangible success and possessions. But happiness comes from within. Ask yourself today, "Who am
I without titles or possessions? Are my actions aligning
with my beliefs?"

# 11

Ask, and it will be given to you;
seek, and you will find;
knock, and it will be opened to you.
For everyone who asks receives,
and he who seeks finds, and to him
who knocks it will be opened.

MATTHEW 7:7-8 NKJV

We know closed mouths don't get fed. The tricky part is
learning to ask God to show you what you need instead
of coming to Him with your master plan.

## 12

But you are a chosen people, a royal priesthood,
a holy nation, God's special possession, that you
may declare the praises of him who called you
out of darkness into his wonderful light.

**1 PETER 2:9 NIV**

Even before you came into the world, God had a specific
purpose for you. You may hit a few potholes on your
journey, but let your faith give you the strength not only
to remember your purpose but also to do your best!

## 13

Lukewarm people don't really want
to be saved from their sin; they want only to
be saved from the penalty of their sin.

**FRANCIS CHAN**

Yikes. Test the temperature of your faith today by
fervently checking your motives. Do your thoughts and
actions come from a pure heart? Open the door to your
heart and ask God to show you His perfect love so that
you may learn from Him.

Praise Him for His grace
and favor to His people in distress.
Praise Him, still the same as ever,
slow to chide, and swift to bless.
Alleluia, alleluia! Glorious in His faithfulness!

"PRAISE, MY SOUL, THE KING OF HEAVEN"
BY HENRY F. LYTE

Alleluia literally means "to praise the Lord." Even though
your mouth sings alleluia, do your actions follow suit?

Enlarge your house; build an addition.
Spread out your home, and spare no expense!
For you will soon be bursting at the seams.

ISAIAH 54:2-3 NLT

In this passage, you are the house. God is expanding
you in every way. Today, begin preparing space for the
blessings He is going to give you. Act as if you have
already received them!

But I have trusted in Your mercy; my heart shall
rejoice in Your salvation. I will sing to the LORD,
because He has dealt bountifully with me.

PSALM 13:5-6 NKJV

When you feel as though anxiety and worry have taken
over, choose to trust in God's unfailing love. Praise
Him in advance for the healing He is going to bring
to your soul.

Friendship is born at that moment
when one person says to another:
"What! You too? I thought I was the only one."

C.S. LEWIS

Your story isn't meant only for you. People around the
world are meant to see that they aren't alone in this
thing called life. Radiate God's love today by sharing
a comforting personal experience with someone you
don't know.

18

Therefore take heed how you hear.
For whoever has, to him more will be given;
and whoever does not have, even what he
seems to have will be taken from him.

LUKE 8:18 NKJV

We all want to be heard, but how often do you listen to understand rather than listen to respond? Listening has the power to change every relationship in your life. Ask God to open your ears to His wisdom, and watch your life transform.

19

For consider Him who endured such hostility
from sinners against Himself, lest you become
weary and discouraged in your souls.

HEBREWS 12:3 NKJV

Sometimes your faith will be tested. Don't be discouraged by the world; instead, be encouraged by God's Word!

Summer and winter and springtime and harvest,
Sun, moon, and stars in their courses above
Join with all nature in manifold witness
To Thy great faithfulness, mercy, and love.

"GREAT IS THY FAITHFULNESS"
BY THOMAS O. CHISHOLM

Open your eyes to see the beauty in all things today.
You have been granted peace through your faith, so
ask God to help you slow down and recognize life's
breathtaking details.

The grass withers, the flower fades,
but the word of our God stands forever.

ISAIAH 40:8 NKJV

Jobs fade, money fades, and even your body will fade.
But the Spirit of God will last forever, so put your hope in
Him alone.

## 22

Just because you help others doesn't mean you
never need help yourself. Doctors can catch colds.
Lawyers can be sued. Police officers can call 911.

SARAH JAKES ROBERTS

As Christians we are called to help, love, and serve
others, but we must remember that we cannot pour from
an empty cup. Fill your cup today with the reminder that
your power comes from God!

## 23

Fear not, for I am with you;
be not dismayed, for I am your God.
I will strengthen you, yes, I will help you,
I will uphold you with My righteous right hand.

ISAIAH 41:10 NKJV

Sometimes we find ourselves worrying about things that
are outside of our control. Choose faith over fear and
allow God's hand to guide you.

For God has not given us a spirit of fear,
but of power and of love and of a sound mind.

2 TIMOTHY 1:7 NKJV

Guess what? Fear is not real—only danger is real. How
will you choose to face danger? Read this scripture again
to remind yourself of the power God gave you!

I hope that my achievements in life shall be these:
that I will have fought for what was right and fair,
that I will have risked for that which mattered,
and that I will have given help to those who were
in need so that I will have left the earth a better
place for what I've done and who I've been.

CARL HOPPE

These aspirations reflect the virtues that we should
strive to embody in our lives as Christians. Remember
that your faith is bigger than you, and your life's actions
should reflect that truth.

# 26

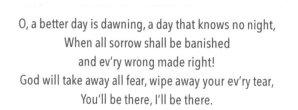

O, a better day is dawning, a day that knows no night,
When all sorrow shall be banished
and ev'ry wrong made right!
God will take away all fear, wipe away your ev'ry tear,
You'll be there, I'll be there.

"A BETTER DAY COMING" BY GRACE WEISER DAVIS

Maybe your year has been off to a rocky start. Be encouraged that better days are coming, and know that God will not abandon you on this journey.

# 27

And do not be conformed to this world,
but be transformed by the renewing of your
mind, that you may prove what is that good
and acceptable and perfect will of God.

ROMANS 12:2 NKJV

The Living Bible puts Paul's instruction more plainly: "Don't copy the behavior and customs of this world." God has a unique calling on your life, and His Word will lead you down the right path.

Now no chastening seems to be joyful
for the present, but painful;
nevertheless, afterward it yields
the peaceable fruit of righteousness
to those who have been trained by it.

HEBREWS 12:11 NKJV

Faith entails discipline, but your perseverance and endurance will pay off. Peace, love, joy, and happiness are waiting for you with open arms!

Choosing to be positive and
having a grateful attitude
is going to determine how
you're going to live your life.

JOEL OSTEEN

You have the power to decide how you want to live your life. Be encouraged to always choose love over evil!

You can suffer the pain of change
or suffer remaining the way you are.

JOYCE MEYER

Have you considered that God is the Picasso of your
pain? Healing takes work, but if you trust in God's plan
for your life, you'll be stronger than ever.

He who believes and is baptized
will be saved;
but he who does not believe
will be condemned.

MARK 16:16 NKJV

Your belief unlocks your freedom. It's not enough to go
through the motions. Ask yourself today: Do you believe
with all of your being?

# 1
## Self-Love

> You watched me as I was being formed in utter seclusion,
> as I was woven together in the dark of the womb.
> You saw me before I was born. Every day of my life
> was recorded in your book. Every moment was
> laid out before a single day had passed.

PSALM 139:15-16 NLT

With Valentine's Day on the 14th, February naturally brings love to the forefront of our minds. You may have plans to spend time with your significant other or family and friends, but even if you don't have anyone to spend this special month with, take comfort in the fact that there is no greater love than God's love.

Psalm 139 is a beautiful depiction of just how much God loves us. When you were in your mother's womb, alone and in the dark, God was there with you. He NEVER left you—and still hasn't. He saw you then and He sees you now. You are perfectly loved in His eyes. No matter what this day may look like for you, remember that He is by your side.

2

It always seems impossible
until it's done.

NELSON MANDELA

Some goals only seem impossible because you don't
know how you're going to reach them. God doesn't want
you to worry about how you will get there. He wants you
to have faith that you can actually achieve the dream!

3

But by the grace of God I am what I am,
and his grace to me was not without effect.
No, I worked harder than all of them—yet not I,
but the grace of God that was with me.

1 CORINTHIANS 15:10 NIV

The gifts God has granted you will help you create your
success. Keep up your hard work today, and remember
that it is only by His grace that you are able to change
the world.

There is a glorious home on high,
Where all is bright and fair;
And they who serve the blessed LORD
Shall dwell forever there.

"A HOME ON HIGH" BY THOMAS C. NEAL

Today, look forward to the joy of spending eternal life with God. Even though we have a home here on Earth, our hearts' home rests with the Savior of the world.

For assuredly, I say to you,
whoever says to this mountain, "Be removed and
be cast into the sea," and does not doubt in his
heart, but believes that those things he says will
be done, he will have whatever he says.

MARK 11:23 NKJV

God has given you the power to change your life circumstances. This means you can call on Heaven and turn your life around. Choose to BELIEVE today!

# 6

Your word is a lamp to my feet,
and a light to my path.

PSALM 119:105 NKJV

Pray for wisdom and discernment today to hear God's voice more clearly. Let His words guide you. You might end up on a path that you never could have imagined.

# 7

Abide in Me, and I in you.
As the branch cannot bear fruit of itself,
unless it abides in the vine,
neither can you, unless you abide in Me.

JOHN 15:4 NKJV

Consider that the branches in this verse are like your veins. Your veins cannot move blood in your body unless they're connected to your heart. God is your heart. He gives you life.

# 8

Trust in the LORD with all your heart,
and lean not on your own understanding;
in all your ways acknowledge Him,
and He shall direct your paths.

**PROVERBS 3:5-6 NKJV**

The word *habits* could stand in for the word *ways* in this passage. Take a moment to acknowledge God in *all* of your habits, good or bad, and allow Him to renew your intentions!

# 9

I know I am weak and sinful,
It comes to me more and more;
But since the dear Savior has bid me come in,
I'll enter the open door.

**"AT THE DOOR" BY URANIA LOCKE BAILEY**

It's a beautiful thing that even though we are filthy with sin, Jesus still wants to hold us in His arms. Let your faith rise today as you rest in the truth that He loves you no matter what.

# 10

The enemy can't take you out
so he's trying to wear you out!

REAL TALK KIM

The evil one knows that the battle was won when Jesus
rose on the third day. You are stronger than you think,
but only difficult circumstances will reveal the extent of
your power to withstand his schemes.

# 11

I can do all things
through Christ who strengthens me.

PHILIPPIANS 4:13 NKJV

As long as you remember where your strength comes
from, you can make it through absolutely anything! But
you don't just need God's strength when it's convenient.
Realize that His strength is what gives you power every
single day.

But seek first the kingdom of God
and His righteousness, and all these
things shall be added to you.

MATTHEW 6:33 NKJV

So often we put our own agenda before God's agenda.
Remember that, as Christians, we are called to do His
work before our own. Put His agenda first today and see
how He blesses your heart.

Life begins at the end of
your comfort zone.

NEALE DONALD WALSCH

When you put your faith in Jesus, life really does begin
at the end of your comfort zone! Let your faith be the
foundation of your dreams and aspirations. What is God
calling you to do? If you're comfortable right now, I can
guarantee He's called you to MORE!

# 14

"For I know the plans I have for you,"
says the Lord. "They are plans for good and not
for disaster, to give you a future and a hope."

JEREMIAH 29:11 NLT

Instead of focusing so much on what the future holds,
allow your faith to strip away that worry so you are able
to enjoy the present moment. Practice present awareness today, because your future is already secured
in Jesus.

# 15

Be still in the presence of the Lord, and wait patiently
for him to act. Don't worry about evil people who
prosper or fret about their wicked schemes.

PSALM 37:7 NLT

Obtaining the life God has called you to live requires a lot
of patience. Choose to show yourself some love today by
giving yourself grace for the process. Ask God to reveal
the bigger lesson He is trying to teach you in this season
of waiting.

O troubled heart, be thou not afraid,
In the LORD thy God, let thy hope be stayed;
He will hear thy cry and will give thee aid,
Whate'er thy cross may be.

"ABLE TO DELIVER" BY FANNY CROSBY

God is with you, so don't let your heart grow heavy with worry. You will make it through the storm. Give God prayers of thanksgiving today and remember that He is always able.

We are not held back by the love
we didn't receive in the past, but by the love
we're not extending in the present.

MARIANNE WILLIAMSON

Whatever your past, you don't live there anymore. Your past doesn't have to define your future. Choose love today.

# 18

Therefore do not cast away your confidence,
which has great reward.

**HEBREWS 10:35 NKJV**

Sometimes we confuse the confidence we put in people
for the confidence we should put in God. You will not
be let down if you truly put all of your confidence in the
Almighty God.

# 19

Have I not commanded you?
Be strong and of good courage;
do not be afraid, nor be dismayed,
for the LORD your God is with you
wherever you go.

**JOSHUA 1:9 NKJV**

Being strong and courageous isn't a choice. God commands us to have confidence in Him. Isn't that refreshing
to know? God feeds our faith and not our insecurities!

# 20

Child of God, oh, hear Him saying,
"In temptation look to me.
E'en when Satan's pow'r seems strongest,
Thy salvation I will be."

"BE STILL" BY KATE ULMER

Instead of letting your emotions rage when you're struggling to resist temptation, tune your ear to God's heart and let your hope come alive. He will guide you out of deep waters and carry you back to the shore.

# 21

If there is a book that you want to read,
but it hasn't been written yet,
you must be the one to write it.

TONI MORRISON

You are the answer to the thing that keeps you up thinking at night. No one else but YOU. Consider this affirmation a nudge from God to go for it!

## 22

The fear of the LORD is the beginning of knowledge,
but fools despise wisdom and instruction.

PROVERBS 1:7 NKJV

If iron sharpens iron, then why can't most people accept healthy criticism? Because pride is in the way. Open your heart to receiving God's teachings on how to become a better person—the lessons may come from an unlikely source.

## 23

Finally, brethren, whatever things are true, whatever
things are noble, whatever things are just, whatever
things are pure, whatever things are lovely, whatever
things are of good report, if there is any virtue and if there
is anything praiseworthy—meditate on these things.

PHILIPPIANS 4:8 NKJV

Take a break from modern life today. Get off social media, ignore celebrity news, and meditate on your faith. You are what you feed your mind, so don't give yourself poison. Feed your mind love, holiness, gentleness, and peace.

Breathe on me, Breath of God,
Fill me with life anew,
That I may love what Thou dost love,
And do what Thou wouldst do.

"BREATHE ON ME, BREATH OF GOD" BY EDWIN HATCH

Genesis says that God breathed into Adam, and he became a living being. Likewise, God has breathed life into you. When you put your faith in God, He will continue to purify your heart!

But the fruit of the Spirit is love, joy, peace, longsuffering, kindness, goodness, faithfulness, gentleness, self-control. Against such there is no law.

GALATIANS 5:22-23 NKJV

Make one of these fruits of the Spirit your intention today. If you choose love, find a creative way to show love to someone or to a few people. If you choose joy, combat every negative thought with a joyful praise. If you choose self-control, stay away from the cookies!

# 26

For God so loved the world
that He gave His only begotten Son,
that whoever believes in Him should not
perish but have everlasting life.

JOHN 3:16 NKJV

When God gave us the amazing gift of Jesus, His great generosity flowed from a stream of perfect love. Allow the full extent of His love to wash over you today and refresh you spiritually.

# 27

Blessed is she who believed,
for there will be a fulfillment of those things
which were told her from the LORD.

LUKE 1:45 NKJV

You are blessed because you believe in the Lord. Don't be lukewarm in your belief. Put ALL of your faith in Him even if you don't understand how He will fulfill His promises to you.

It's easy to be common.
The pressure comes when you decide
to be uncommon.

JOEL OSTEEN

As a believer, you are meant to stand out so that God's love can stand out! Don't be afraid of your uniqueness. Be bold and be YOU in the name of Jesus.

I lay down and slept;
I awoke, for the LORD sustained me. I will not be afraid of ten thousands of people who have set themselves against me all around.

PSALM 3:5-6 NKJV

Have you ever gone to sleep and everything in your life seemed to be okay? Then you woke up the next morning to have everything go wrong? The next time, remember: You were protected before, and you are still protected now!

# 1

# Shame

> For the Scripture says,
> "Whoever believes in Him will not
> be put to shame."

ROMANS 10:11 NKJV

Romans 10 touches on how drastically the means of the world's salvation was transformed by Jesus. Before Jesus came, people just tried to keep the law of Moses. They believed that as long as they didn't break the rules, they would be right with God. But after Jesus died for us, we learned that the true way of faith is believing in your heart that Jesus is Lord.

As believers, we have an amazing opportunity to experience what Jesus's perfect love is like. We are already forgiven. Where God's love is, there is NO shame. You don't have to cover up your scars, because His blood has already washed them away. If you have been struggling with shame, say this prayer: "God, I have been feeling unworthy of Your love. I am shameful for what I have done, and I am in need of Your forgiveness. Heal my heart as I come back to where I started. Help me be free again. Amen."

Set your mind on things above,
not on things on the earth.

COLOSSIANS 3:2 NKJV

Setting your mind on the spiritual—going beyond the superficial—gives you a higher personal standard to strive for. This standard doesn't mean you are better than anyone. It just means that you understand where true peace and fulfillment come from.

O what is thy burden so heavy today,
That gloom fills thy spirit and joy flees away?
Thy faults rise before thee and fill with dismay,
Go carry thy burden to Jesus.

"CARRY IT ALL TO JESUS" BY HENRY J. ZELLEY

You were not meant to carry the burdens of life alone. Cry out to Jesus today and ask Him to lift the pain from your shoulders. Freedom is calling your name!

4

Don't fear opposition.
Expect it. And use it as an opportunity
to fuel your growth.

STEVEN FURTICK

When your enemies oppose you, learn to elevate your mentality rather than deteriorate under your insecurities. God said that you are the salt and light of the world (Matthew 5:13–16), so let your faith fill you with confidence!

5

For whatever things were written before
were written for our learning,
that we through the patience and comfort
of the Scriptures might have hope.

ROMANS 15:4 NKJV

God gave us what we need in the Bible, so don't take scripture for granted! Use His Word to change your heart AND the world!

Now to Him who is able to do exceedingly
abundantly above all that we ask or think,
according to the power that works in us.

EPHESIANS 3:20 NKJV

God does not have to use us to spread His glory in the
world, but He chooses to use us anyway. Take a second
to really think about that. He can do so much more than
your mind can conceptualize, and the best part about His
master plan is that He is going to use YOU to achieve it.
Be glad!

The Savior is dearer to me every day,
The closer I live to Him;
And brighter His glory illumines my way,
The closer I live to Him.

"CLOSER TO JESUS" BY RUFUS H. MCDANIEL

Your trials should draw you ever more near to Jesus.
Trials don't always mean trouble—sometimes they mean
God is calling you home to Him.

# 8

Peace I leave with you.
My peace I give to you;
not as the world gives do I give to you.
Let not your heart be troubled,
neither let it be afraid.

**JOHN 14:27 NKJV**

We are troubled and afraid because we look for peace of heart and mind in the world. Yoga, vacations, and bubble baths can't bring you inner peace without God. Reassess today and recognize that He has gifted us with peace from above.

# 9

Spread love everywhere you go.
Let no one ever come to you
without leaving happier.

**MOTHER TERESA**

Encourage someone today with a random act of kindness. The world needs your love!

In the day when I cried out,
You answered me, and made me bold
with strength in my soul.

PSALM 138:3 NKJV

This verse demonstrates that God hears us. Your cries
don't go unnoticed. Reach into the well of your soul and
remember that your strength is found in Him.

God loves each of us
as if there were only one of us.

AUGUSTINE

Do not feel jealous of your neighbor or of their relationship with God. Trust His Word and believe in God's
perfect love for you.

Thus says the LORD of hosts:
"Return to Me . . . and I will return to you."

ZECHARIAH 1:3 NKJV

No matter how far you may stray, God will always allow you to turn back to Him. Accept forgiveness and repent. You can always try again.

God never said that the journey would be easy,
but He did say that
the arrival would be worthwhile.

MAX LUCADO

God also said that "no weapon formed against you shall prosper" (Isaiah 54:17 NKJV). He didn't say that the weapons wouldn't exist or pose a threat. Find beauty in the journey and set your faith on what is to come.

Of such a one I will boast;
yet of myself I will not boast,
except in my infirmities.

2 CORINTHIANS 12:5 NKJV

Today, instead of speaking about the amazing opportunities you have been granted or the great amount of success you have achieved, speak about how God renewed your spirit during times of weakness.

But He knows the way that I take;
when He has tested me,
I shall come forth as gold.

JOB 23:10 NKJV

If you ask God for peace, He will put you in a circumstance that tests your patience. If you pray for strength, be prepared to endure some pressure. The Lord tests your will to make you more resilient. Don't be afraid; rise to the occasion!

# 16

God will meet you where you are
in order to take you
where He wants you to go.

TONY EVANS

The God of the universe stoops to your level out of love, not pity. Wherever you are in life, He is on the journey with you. Set your eyes on Him and let your fear fade away.

# 17

But He needed to go through Samaria.

JOHN 4:4 NKJV

Jesus needed to go through Samaria on His way to Galilee because He needed to teach the Samaritans, who had been misguided in their faith. Let this remind you that Jesus has placed you where you are for a divine reason. Don't miss out on your mission because you're too busy worrying about the final destination!

Our greatest fear should not be of failure
but of succeeding at things in life
that don't really matter.

FRANCIS CHAN

Does your job matter more than your happiness? Does a toxic relationship feel safer than taking a risk on experiencing true confidence and self-love? Redefine what true success looks like for you, and allow your faith to guide your heart to true peace.

You are the only Bible
some unbelievers will ever read.

JOHN MACARTHUR

Your faith is a light in the world! Where darkness lies, you have the opportunity to spread love, joy, and tenderness. Will you let your faith speak for you today?

Be anxious for nothing,
but in everything by prayer and supplication,
with thanksgiving, let your requests
be made known to God.

PHILIPPIANS 4:6 NKJV

God is concerned with your needs and wholeheartedly wants to hear them. Don't come to God complaining. Come to Him with praise and faith, knowing that He has everything you need.

You gain strength, and courage, and confidence
by each experience in which you really stop
to look fear in the face. . . . You must do
that which you think you cannot.

ELEANOR ROOSEVELT

Fear is a liar. The next time fear presents itself in your life, challenge it with what the Word says is true. Where there is God's perfect love, there is NO fear!

Refrain from anger and turn from wrath;
do not fret—it leads only to evil.

PSALM 37:8 NIV

Have you ever said something when you were upset that you later regretted? Being angry only makes matters worse. Take a shot at choosing peace and forgiveness today, regardless of the outcome.

We are all faced with a series
of great opportunities brilliantly disguised
as impossible situations.

CHARLES R. SWINDOLL

Your faith should be the fire that burns negative attitudes! Every day is an opportunity to achieve something greater than you did yesterday.

# 24

He sets on high those who are lowly,
and those who mourn are lifted to safety.

JOB 5:11 NKJV

Going through a difficult time is never easy, but your attitude and perspective will define the outcome of your journey. God's Word shows us how to abide in Him and act on our faith. He will lift you high in due time!

# 25

As the deer pants for the water brooks,
so pants my soul for You, O God.

PSALM 42:1 NKJV

God has placed eternity in our hearts so our souls will forever thirst for Him. Let this verse be your anthem today, and have hope in the knowledge that He will fill you up.

And there is no creature hidden from His sight,
but all things are naked and open to the eyes
of Him to whom we must give account.

HEBREWS 4:13 NKJV

It might sound scary that God sees everything tangible
and intangible, but this scripture is intended to motivate you in a positive way rather than make you feel
ashamed. Assess your intentions today. Are you making
decisions from a pure heart?

He who dwells in the secret place of the Most High shall abide
under the shadow of the Almighty. I will say of the LORD,
"He is my refuge and my fortress; my God, in Him I will trust."

PSALM 91:1-2 NKJV

Who do you run to when things are difficult? Do you
come to God in prayer before you vent to a friend or
family member? You can trust God above anyone. Try
coming to Him during troubled times and watch how
He covers you with peace.

## 28

For if you remain completely silent at this time,
relief and deliverance will arise for the Jews from
another place, but you and your father's house
will perish. Yet who knows whether you have
come to the kingdom for such a time as this?

ESTHER 4:14 NKJV

The time is NOW. Tomorrow is not promised. What are
you waiting for? You were created for this specific time
in the world!

MARCH

## 29

Be faithful in small things because it is
in them that your strength lies.

MOTHER TERESA

"Small things" include the daily conversations you
have with yourself. Is your faith guiding you to speak
kindly to yourself, or do you fall into negative self-talk?
Take a moment to assess your confidence and find the
strength to love!

And you shall love the LORD your God
with all your heart, with all your soul,
with all your mind, and with all your strength.
This is the first commandment.

MARK 12:30 NKJV

Love is at the essence of who we are. The more you
learn to love God, the more you will discover who you
are in Him. Then nothing will be able to bring you down
in this world.

There is no one who is
insignificant in the purpose of God.

ALISTAIR BEGG

Self-condemnation can make you feel like you don't
matter. Instead of choosing self-condemnation, choose
to believe the truth that God thought you were worth
sending His Son to die for you.

# 1

# Worship

> But they found the stone
> rolled away from the tomb.
> Then they went in and did not find
> the body of the LORD Jesus.

LUKE 24:2-3 NKJV

Luke 24 describes what happened when Jesus rose from the grave. Can you imagine the emotions people were experiencing when they realized that everything Jesus had said would happen had actually happened? Confusion was their natural initial response, but wasn't joy, jubilation, and ecstatic celebration in order? After all, the Savior had overcome death and paid the wages of sin for everyone!

The month of April has so many beautiful holidays that represent faith in Jesus. With April comes Palm Sunday, Good Friday, the end of Lent, and Easter. I want to encourage you to take on a heart of worship this month. Worship goes beyond how we sing praises. Worship should be your heart's posture!

Blessed is the man who walks not
in the counsel of the ungodly,
nor stands in the path of sinners,
nor sits in the seat of the scornful;
but his delight is in the law of the LORD.

PSALM 1:1-2 NKJV

What makes you happy? Does your happiness come
from a place of selfishness or a place of godliness? Make
finding delight in God's Word your life's mission!

Cause every task of your day
to be a sacred ministry to the LORD.
However mundane your duties,
for you they are a sacrament.

RICHARD FOSTER

God doesn't waste anything. He has put purpose in
every step you take, big or small. Let your faith be the
cornerstone of your intentions today.

4

Ask me, and I will make
the nations your inheritance,
the ends of the earth your possession.

PSALM 2:8 NIV

God already knows what you need, but He wants you to
have enough courage to ask. The Word tells us that if we
ask in good faith, we shall receive!

5

We are bound for Canaan land,
Tenting by the way;
Who shall lead us on the road?
Choose your king today.

"DARE TO STAND LIKE JOSHUA" BY C.M. ROBINSON

God has destined you for something great in your life.
Along the way there will be potholes and detours, but
will you continue to choose the King to lead you to
still waters?

6

Salvation belongs to the LORD.
Your blessing is upon Your people.

PSALM 3:8 NKJV

Be reminded that your success is God-given—not
self-driven. All blessings come from the Lord, and
we owe Him our praise!

7

I will both lie down in peace, and sleep;
for You alone, O LORD,
make me dwell in safety.

PSALM 4:8 NKJV

Even if you can't see past your struggles right now, trust
His Word. It assures us that we can still have peace and
rest in His safety. Let go today.

**APRIL**

# 8

Work becomes worship when you
dedicate it to God and perform it with
an awareness of his presence.

RICK WARREN

Assess your motivations and dedicate your work to the
Lord today by asking Him to guide you with His presence
and wisdom. That is true worship!

**APRIL**

# 9

Know that the LORD, He is God;
it is He who has made us,
and not we ourselves; we are His people
and the sheep of His pasture.

PSALM 100:3 NKJV

This Psalm perfectly illustrates what it means to die and
take up the cross. Never forget that everything we have
was given to us by God! Praise Him by being a living
reminder of His Good Word today.

The closer you get to the truth,
the clearer becomes the beauty, and the more
you will find worship welling up within you.

N. T. WRIGHT

Take time today to meditate on what truth looks like in
your life right now. Ask God to paint a clearer picture of
what His truth means for your life.

I will make Your name to be remembered
in all generations; therefore the people
shall praise You forever and ever.

PSALM 45:17 NKJV

Are you living to make Him famous on Earth or are you
striving to become famous? What are you doing that is
making God's name known?

# 12

Dwell in me, O blessed Spirit!
How I need Thy help divine!
In the way of life eternal,
Keep, O keep this heart of mine.

"DWELL IN ME, O BLESSED SPIRIT"
BY FANNY CROSBY

If you aren't careful to guard your heart, life sure can beat it up. The beautiful thing is that you can always be healed from the inside out with the work of the Holy Spirit.

# 13

The LORD will give strength to His people;
the LORD will bless His people with peace.

PSALM 29:11 NKJV

You have access to everything you need internally. The key is putting yourself in the position to receive it. Spend some quiet time today with Him so that He can lift your head high.

I will bless the LORD at all times;
His praise shall continually be in my mouth.
My soul shall make its boast in the LORD; the humble
shall hear of it and be glad. Oh, magnify the LORD
with me, and let us exalt His name together.

PSALM 34:1-3 NKJV

The Word says that we should "pray without ceasing"
(1 Thessalonians 5:17 NKJV). Be challenged today
to pray more than you normally do—maybe even ask
a friend or family member to join you. Whatever you do,
use your prayers to praise God!

It is the pleasing of God
that is at the heart of worship.

R. C. SPROUL

Worship is how you live your life. Surrender yourself
completely and prioritize pleasing God not only through
your words but also through your intentions, conversations, and the way you love. Let Him cleanse your heart!

# 16

In God I have put my trust; I will not be
afraid. What can man do to me?

**PSALM 56:11 NKJV**

People may try to hurt you, but God is protecting your
soul. They can't reach the intangible! Let your faith well
up inside of you today, and trust that God will shield you
to your core.

# 17

Worship has been misunderstood as something
that arises from a feeling which "comes upon you,"
but it is vital that we understand that
it is rooted in a conscious act of the will,
to serve and obey the LORD Jesus Christ.

**GRAHAM KENDRICK**

God gave you free will, and what you do with it is the
measure of your faith and your worship. How will you
serve God through love?

# 18

I acknowledged my sin to You, and my iniquity I have not hidden. I said, "I will confess my transgressions to the LORD," and You forgave the iniquity of my sin.

**PSALM 32:5 NKJV**

The freedom that comes with forgiveness is yours when you confess openly to the Lord. Remember that what is hidden cannot be healed and that because Jesus died, you are already forgiven! Let the light of His truth shine over your sins. Freedom is calling!

# 19

Father in the morning unto thee I pray,
Let Thy loving kindness keep me thro' this day.
At the busy noontide, press'd with work and care,
Then I'll wait with Jesus till He hear my pray'r.

**"EVER WILL I PRAY" BY ANNIE CUMMINGS**

Don't get caught up entirely in to-do lists today. Make time for Jesus, even if it's just five minutes during your lunch break. You'll feel refreshed and ready to finish your day strong.

# 20

Let us go into His tabernacle;
let us worship at His footstool.

PSALM 132:7 NKJV

Where you worship can impact how you worship. Do you
have a quiet place where you can get into His presence?
Seek out places that allow you freedom and solitude.

# 21

Worship is the proper response of all moral,
sentient beings to God, ascribing all honor
and worth to their Creator-God precisely
because he is worthy, delightfully so.

D.A. CARSON

He is FOREVER worthy of your praises. Let your faith
remind you of this beautiful truth today!

Thus I will bless You while I live;
I will lift up my hands in Your name.

PSALM 63:4 NKJV

Sometimes in worship, words can't express what we want to say to God, and we need to express our faith through our bodies instead!

His perfect holiness, by definition,
assures us that our words can't contain Him.
Isn't it a comfort to worship a God
we cannot exaggerate?

FRANCIS CHAN

Let your faith rise today, knowing that God is bigger than you can ever imagine—yet He loves you so intimately!

# 24

My mouth shall speak wisdom, and the meditation of my heart shall give understanding. I will incline my ear to a proverb; I will disclose my dark saying on the harp.

### PSALM 49:3-4 NKJV

Do you find your heart and mind filled with worry? Meditation can provide enlightenment and help you accept the things you don't yet comprehend. Seek peace by focusing on God's glory and resting in His presence.

# 25

Ever near, ever near, Jesus blessed Saviour;
Why should mortals doubt or fear,
Blessed with Thy favor.
Ever near, ever near, think not 'tis tomorrow;
Jesus wipes the present tear,
From the eye of sorrow.

### "EVER NEAR" BY JOHN H. KURZENKNABE

Sometimes we must go through pain today so that tomorrow can be brighter. Sometimes the Lord must break our will so that we can fulfill a higher calling.

When my spirit grows faint within me,
it is you who watch over my way.

PSALM 142:3 NIV

Let David's experience in the cave be an example to you.
In his darkest times, he prayed and relied on his faith to
see him through. Revive your weary soul by reminding
yourself that God is watching over you.

Nothing teaches us about the preciousness
of the Creator as much as when we learn
the emptiness of everything else.

CHARLES SPURGEON

When you realize that your belongings have no significant value, you will begin to understand the true beauty
of the things you can't touch.

# 28

O my soul, you have said to the LORD,
"You are my LORD,
my goodness is nothing apart from You."

PSALM 16:2 NKJV

Without God, our victories mean nothing. Remember that He is the reason you are able to do great things. Give thanks and be glad!

# 29

You never go away from us,
yet we have difficulty in returning to You.
Come, LORD, stir us up and call us back.
Kindle and seize us. Be our fire and our
sweetness. Let us love. Let us run.

AUGUSTINE

God's love truly is unconditional. It is so comforting to know that He never leaves us, and by our faith we are able to come back to Him when we wander away.

# 30

I said, "I will watch my ways and
keep my tongue from sin;
I will put a muzzle on my mouth while
in the presence of the wicked."

**PSALM 39:1 NIV**

There is power in your words! In fact, the careless things we say often prevent us from achieving the life to which God has called us. Consider your words carefully, and strive to speak life instead of death.

MAY

# 1

## Gentleness

> Take my yoke upon you and learn from me,
> for I am gentle and humble in heart, and
> you will find rest for your souls.

MATTHEW 11:29 NIV

There is cruelty and evil in this world, and it can beat you down. Even as we try to recover, the residue of deep pain can linger in our souls. So, how do we move forward? Turn to the book of Matthew, when Jesus was speaking to a crowd of people and giving a prayer of thanksgiving. He knew that here on Earth, the world would torment our souls, but He offered us a hiding place. He gave us the key to making it through the journey of life: to take His yoke and learn from Him.

Even though Jesus was beaten as He made the walk to his imminent death—even though He was tormented on a level none of us will understand—he spoke with such gentleness. Jesus's example serves as a reminder of how we should carry ourselves. Regardless of how beaten up you might get, let gentleness come from your lips. Gentleness yields rest for your soul, because you know where your hope lies. Trust, rejoice, be glad!

For the LORD gives wisdom;
from His mouth come knowledge
and understanding.

PROVERBS 2:6 NKJV

If we open our mouths and ask for wisdom, He will give it to us. Don't let the fear of the unknown stop you from pursuing all that He has for you.

But just as your body needs sleep,
your soul needs time to rest in God.
To learn more about Him. To talk to Him.
To worship and praise Him. To fellowship
with other brothers and sisters.

CRAIG GROESCHEL

The best soul food you can give yourself is meditation with God, rest in God, and hope in God. His love is rejuvenating!

4

Bear one another's burdens,
and so fulfill the law of Christ.

GALATIANS 6:2 NKJV

We are not meant to walk alone. Spread God's love
today, and take some time to check on your friends
and family!

5

For us the crown of thorns he bore;
For us to robe of scorn He wore;
He conquer'd death, and rent the grave,
And lives again our souls to save.

"FOR YOU AND ME" BY FANNY CROSBY

When Jesus rose from the grave, He granted you a safe
haven of love and peace forever. Have a little faith today,
knowing that He who started a good work in you will
finish it!

Go therefore and make disciples of all the
nations, baptizing them in the name of the Father
and of the Son and of the Holy Spirit.

MATTHEW 28:19 NKJV

If you're questioning your purpose, look no further. We
are ALL called to make Jesus known on Earth by showing love in our words and actions.

When you are running toward Christ,
you are freed up to serve, love, and give thanks
without guilt, worry, or fear. As long as
you are running, you're safe.

FRANCIS CHAN

Check your compass today. In which direction are you
running? Toward Christ, or away from Him? Let your faith
lead you toward God's will for your life. Don't let sin lead
you astray!

8

For all have sinned
and fall short of the glory of God.

ROMANS 3:23 NKJV

Don't set yourself up for failure by making perfection
a goal. Let this verse remind you that the only perfect
thing in the world is God's perfect love!

9

For wisdom is better than rubies,
and all the things one may desire
cannot be compared with her.

PROVERBS 8:11 NKJV

Knowing WHAT to do with your assets is better than
actually having them. Don't flaunt your blessings.
Wisdom is glorifying God with how He has blessed you.
Be wise with your will today!

'Tis sweet in the presence of Jesus to dwell,
Thro' troubles and trials annoy,
To constantly feel His approval and smile:
In this there is fullness of joy!

"FULLNESS OF JOY" BY M.L. HERR

You have the stamp of approval in Jesus's eyes. Do not
fear that He is disappointed or angry with you. That's
just self-condemnation luring you into the bondage of
your own mind. Let your faith free you today, and know
that He is pleased with you!

Since we are surrounded by so great a cloud of witnesses, let
us lay aside every weight, and the sin which so easily ensnares
us, and let us run with endurance the race that is set before us.

HEBREWS 12:1 NKJV

The pace of your race may be different than another's,
but the principle is the same for everyone. Strip yourself
of the weight that slows you—excuses, toxic relationships,
negative self-talk—and run to the beat of God's heart!

God directs His people not simply to worship but to sing His praises "before the nations." We are called not simply to communicate the gospel to nonbelievers; we must also intentionally celebrate the gospel before them.

TIMOTHY J. KELLER

Your actions may show one thing, but your intentions may reveal something else. Ask yourself: "Am I putting on a performance before the nations, or am I pure in heart about being the salt and light of the world?" (See Matthew 5:13–16 NKJV.)

In the beginning
God created the heavens and the earth.

GENESIS 1:1 NKJV

In the beginning, God *created*. Because you are made in His image, you too have the power to create! Use the skills and gifts with which He has blessed you to create the life you want to live.

Then Jesus spoke to them again, saying,
"I am the light of the world. He who follows Me shall
not walk in darkness, but have the light of life."

JOHN 8:12 NKJV

When you walk with Jesus, darkness doesn't stand
a chance! Let this truth spark your hope to come alive.

From ev'ry stormy wind that blows,
From ev'ry swelling tide of woes,
There is a calm, a sure retreat:
'Tis found beneath the mercy seat.

"FROM EVERY STORMY WIND THAT BLOWS"
BY HUGH STOWELL

When the disciples were on a boat together in the
middle of a severe storm, they had little faith (see
Mark 4:35–41). Even though Jesus, the Savior of the
world, was with them, they still didn't believe they were
safe! Have faith that His mercy has you wrapped up in
His safety!

# 16

But you shall receive power when the Holy Spirit has come upon you; and you shall be witnesses to Me in Jerusalem, and in all Judea and Samaria, and to the end of the earth.

ACTS 1:8 NKJV

The power to overcome life's difficulties became yours when the Holy Spirit made a home in your heart. God will not do for us what we can do for ourselves! Speak LIFE over your circumstances and watch how things shift today.

# 17

God has a purpose behind every problem. He uses circumstances to develop our character. In fact, he depends more on circumstances to make us like Jesus than he depends on our reading the Bible.

RICK WARREN

How crazy is it that God uses our mess to teach us what is already written? Consider it true love and grace that He meets us where we are and doesn't condemn us for seeking Him in the Word first!

All Scripture is given by inspiration of God,
and is profitable for doctrine, for reproof, for
correction, for instruction in righteousness.

2 TIMOTHY 3:16 NKJV

Scripture will strengthen not only your relationship
with God but also your relationship with yourself. Let
your faith be your catalyst for self-
reflection, and strive to be better than you were
yesterday.

While as Christians we journey to the mansions of light,
Many trials await us, many battles to fight;
But whatever may trouble, we have but this to do;
"Cast all your care on Jesus for He careth for you."

"FOR HE CARETH FOR YOU" BY H.B. BENGLE

Putting our full faith in Jesus is so much easier said than
done, but doing so can be simpler than you think. God is
bigger than your problems. The question is, is your faith
big enough to trust that He will free you?

# 20

That if you confess with your mouth the LORD
Jesus and believe in your heart that God has
raised Him from the dead, you will be saved.

ROMANS 10:9 NKJV

Apply the same strength of will to your life that's
described in this verse. Knowing anything is possible,
let your faith push you to be the best version of yourself
for God, your loved ones, and yourself.

# 21

For the wages of sin is death,
but the gift of God is eternal life
in Christ Jesus our LORD.

ROMANS 6:23 NKJV

Sin had to be paid for, and because God loved us so
much, He paid the steep price for us with His only begotten Son. Embrace the gift of freedom today by not being
bound by life's circumstances.

Spending time with God is the key to our strength and success in all areas of life. Be sure that you never try to work God into your schedule, but always work your schedule around Him.

JOYCE MEYER

Is God your top priority? Before your loved ones, before yourself, before your job—God should remain the center of your life.

But as many as received Him,
to them He gave the right to become children
of God, to those who believe in His name.

JOHN 1:12 NKJV

When the wages of sin were paid, you were granted birthright status in the family of God! This means that no matter what your earthly situation is, your spiritual "situation" takes precedence over all. Rejoice and be glad!

# 24

Sometimes you must stand still
in order to get moving to
where God wants you to go.

D.A. MCBRIDE

Standing still doesn't necessarily mean giving up. There is purpose in the "pause." Ask God for discernment today to recognize where He is guiding you.

# 25

And we know that all things work together
for good to those who love God,
to those who are the called
according to His purpose.

ROMANS 8:28 NKJV

This scripture doesn't say only SOME things work together. It says that ALL things work together for your good. Have hope in the knowledge that no matter what happens, the universe is on your side.

We need never shout across the spaces to an
absent God. He is nearer than our own soul,
closer than our most secret thoughts.

A.W. TOZER

Sometimes we feel like God isn't near us in our pain.
But never forget—the Creator of the universe is always
resting inside of your heart. Let the Holy Spirit comfort
you today.

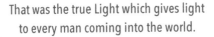

That was the true Light which gives light
to every man coming into the world.

JOHN 1:9 NKJV

In this verse, John was expressing that Jesus is the true
Light who gives all of us light in our souls. Be encouraged today that we will continue to be redeemed by His
light and kindness!

## MAY

## 28

Do all the good you can. By all the means you can. In all the ways you can. In all the places you can. At all the times you can. To all the people you can. As long as ever you can.

JOHN WESLEY

Make this quote your life's mantra! It captures what spreading God's love looks like here on Earth. YOU are the vessel for change, so let your faith lead your heart's intention!

## MAY

## 29

Then God said, "Let Us make man in Our image, according to Our likeness; let them have dominion over the fish of the sea, over the birds of the air, and over the cattle, over all the earth and over every creeping thing that creeps on the earth."

GENESIS 1:26 NKJV

Your heavenly Father created you in His image! Let this truth refresh your perception of yourself today. No, you are not God, but the power of His love flows through you. You are everything you need to be because He said that you are!

True faith means holding nothing back.
It means putting every hope
in God's fidelity to His promises.

FRANCIS CHAN

Take a moment today and ask God to open your heart
to see where you're holding back. God wants to be wel-
comed into every area of your life. Has your faith been
lukewarm lately?

Through wisdom a house is built,
and by understanding it is established;
by knowledge the rooms are filled with
all precious and pleasant riches.

PROVERBS 24:3-4 NKJV

Wisdom is your foundation; understanding is your means
of growth and maturity, and applying knowledge, through
prayer, is your tool for a prosperous life!

# 1

# Sacrifice

> Greater love has no one than this, than to
> lay down one's life for his friends.

**JOHN 15:13 NKJV**

Jesus is not only our teacher—He is our friend. He paid the price for all of humanity because He loves us. His was the ultimate sacrifice that anyone can make for a person they care about. Self-care is important, but in this age of social media when "selfies" are taking center stage, we have a problem with selfishness. Our society promotes pride, greed, and false humility, and sometimes it's hard to escape these ills.

I challenge you to try to sacrifice something small for someone else once a week this month or even once a day. Instead of buying lunch at work, pack a lunch for yourself and buy one for a friend. When doing your budget, set aside funds to donate to charity. Stretch yourself in every way possible to be more like Jesus. Sacrifice means putting personal emotions aside, being bigger than yourself, and prioritizing others. Be more like Jesus this month and watch your faith blossom!

Take the world, but give me Jesus,
All its joys are but a name;
But His love abideth ever,
Through eternal years the same.

"GIVE ME JESUS" BY FANNY CROSBY

Let these lyrics be your praise today! Find joy in the unattainable things and share that joy with someone else. The Father willingly gave you Jesus. Is that gift enough for you?

But God showed his great love for us by sending Christ to die for us while we were still sinners.

ROMANS 5:8 NLT

Even when He knew we would continue to sin, the plan never changed. This unwavering commitment speaks volumes to the love God has for His children. Be redeemed by His perfect love!

# 4

God is most glorified in us
when we are most satisfied in Him.

**JOHN PIPER**

God isn't most glorified when we get recognized, promoted, or even married. He is most glorified in us when we know that He is the only true satisfaction we will ever find.

# 5

You are a child of God, destined for glory,
and called to do great things in His Name.

**PAUL DAVID WASHER**

Never let anyone diminish your value. The CEO of a company and the janitor of a school are valued and loved equally in God's eyes. He has great things in store for you that no one can take away.

And Jesus came and spoke to them, saying,
"All authority has been given to Me
in heaven and on earth."

MATTHEW 28:18 NKJV

Don't blur the distinction between the authority of
earthly leaders and God's authority. Be reminded today
that good leadership is about making God's love—not
your name—known.

They who seek the throne of grace,
Find that throne in every place;
If we live a life of prayer,
God is present everywhere.

"GOD IS PRESENT EVERYWHERE" BY OLIVER HOLDEN

Sometimes we seek God in a certain place only to find
out that He is more present than we ever knew. Let your
prayer open your eyes today!

Jesus answered and said to him,
"Most assuredly, I say to you, unless one is born
again, he cannot see the kingdom of God."

**JOHN 3:3 NKJV**

We can die to ourselves and be born again. Take a
moment to rededicate your life to God today for
a fresh start.

We sinned for no reason
but an incomprehensible lack of love,
and He saved us for no reason but an
incomprehensible excess of love.

**PETER KREEFT**

We live here on Earth because of an incomprehensible
gift of grace. Even though you may not understand, fall
into His perfect love and be redeemed.

The thief does not come except to steal,
and to kill, and to destroy. I have come
that they may have life, and that they
may have it more abundantly.

JOHN 10:10 NKJV

The evil one wants to trick you into thinking that God
has abandoned you in the midst of your struggles and
that you should just give up. But when Jesus died on the
cross, He won the battle for us forever. Know that your
life is already saved!

As long as you do things for God,
you are a Hall of Famer in heaven's list.

RICK WARREN

Great success on Earth is amazing and bound to happen
when you work hard, but remember that the fruits of
your labor will eventually fade. Find hope in the things
that remain forever in Heaven!

So the Word became human
and made His home among us.
He was full of unfailing love and faithfulness.
And we have seen His glory, the glory of
the Father's one and only Son.

JOHN 1:14 NLT

When things get hard, never forget that God made Himself human so that He could meet us where we are. He has experienced every pain that we have, and He has given us the power to overcome!

We never grow closer to God
when we just live life. It takes deliberate
pursuit and attentiveness.

FRANCIS CHAN

Your intentionality defines the depth of your relationship with God. Seek Him eagerly and He will meet you!

# 14

Oh hearts that ache, and bleed and break,
God knows the depths of all thy woes,
He will Himself, thy burdens take,
And shield thee from the heaviest blows.

"GOD KNOWS THY NEED" BY ANONYMOUS

When you feel like the world is against you, and you just can't take anymore, think of Jesus on the cross. He endured worse pain than you will ever feel so that you can be free!

# 15

All the believers devoted themselves
to the apostles' teaching, and to fellowship,
and to sharing in meals (including the
LORD's Supper), and to prayer.

ACTS 2:42 NLT

Scripture shows us that faith is stronger in community. You are who you surround yourself with, so find other believers who will push you toward Jesus and challenge you to grow!

# 16

Not by works of righteousness
which we have done, but according to His
mercy He saved us, through the washing of
regeneration and renewing of the Holy Spirit.

**TITUS 3:5 NKJV**

Jesus's mercy and grace have allowed us to be in communion with Him. Remember that it is only through Him that we are able!

# 17

Outside of Christ, I am weak;
in Christ, I am strong.

**WATCHMAN NEE**

As long as you remember this truth, you're allowing God's power to remain the cornerstone of your life, and that power will make you stronger than ever.

Let not your heart be troubled;
you believe in God, believe also in Me.

JOHN 14:1 NKJV

Jesus wants your faith in Him to set you free from the world! Put your earthly disappointments and heartaches aside and take comfort in the immeasurable joy He has secured for you in Heaven.

And He Himself gave some to be apostles,
some prophets, some evangelists, and some pastors
and teachers, for the equipping of the saints
for the work of ministry,
for the edifying of the body of Christ.

EPHESIANS 4:11–12 NKJV

God didn't leave us alone to figure out how to maneu-ver through life by ourselves. He has given us pastors, teachers, and prophets to illuminate His Word in the world and to encourage our faith to grow!

# 20

What you are is God's gift to you,
what you become is your gift to God.

### HANS URS VON BALTHASAR

One way we glorify God is by using our gifts to spread His light. Are you sleeping on your gifts or using them to spread the gospel?

# 21

Come to Me,
all you who labor and are heavy laden,
and I will give you rest.

### MATTHEW 11:28 NKJV

Your burdens are not meant for you to carry. Jesus is happy to take the weight off your shoulders. Run to Him because rest is waiting for you!

## 22

Therefore, having been justified by faith,
we have peace with God
through our LORD Jesus Christ.

**ROMANS 5:1 NKJV**

Because you believe, you already have peace in your
soul. Now you just need to access it. Take a moment to
thank God for this gift.

---

## 23

In all that befalls me, I know Jesus cares;
Great is His mercy toward me;
He lightens each burden, each sorrow He shares;
Great is His mercy toward me.

**"GREAT IS HIS MERCY" BY MAUD FRAZER**

Don't blame God for the poor actions of others. He cares
for your life and wants you to find hope in Him. Trust that
He will calm your heart and rest your spirit through trials.

# 24

Thou hast made us for thyself, O LORD,
and our heart is restless
until it finds its rest in thee.

**AUGUSTINE**

God made us for Himself and no one else. Feel empowered to stop giving your heart to people who don't
deserve it. Your heart already has a home—because
of your faith, you belong with Jesus.

# 25

For I am not ashamed of the gospel of Christ,
for it is the power of God to salvation
for everyone who believes,
for the Jew first and also for the Greek.

**ROMANS 1:16 NKJV**

Ask God to show you new ways to be bold in your faith.
Never let the world dim your light.

The Christian shoemaker does his duty
not by putting little crosses on the shoes,
but by making good shoes, because God is
interested in good craftsmanship.

MARTIN LUTHER

Because God crafted us so uniquely and so exceptionally,
He expects nothing less from us. In all things, give God
your best today!

If we confess our sins,
He is faithful and just to forgive us our sins and
to cleanse us from all unrighteousness.

1 JOHN 1:9 NKJV

Forgiveness comes when we confess! Cast out the
darkness in your life, and let your faith lead you to
redemption.

**JUNE**

# 28

Prayer is the portal that brings the power of heaven down to earth. It is kryptonite to the enemy and to all his ploys against you.

PRISCILLA SHIRER

Prayer is your key to freedom. What you speak out of your mouth unto God has the power to drastically alter your life. Let your faith give you confidence to fight the enemy!

**JUNE**

# 29

Therefore, if anyone is in Christ,
he is a new creation;
old things have passed away; behold,
all things have become new.

2 CORINTHIANS 5:17 NKJV

When you come to Christ, He forgives and forgets! Challenge yourself to forgive someone else. Let go of the past and make room for love, peace, and joy.

Now faith is the substance
of things hoped for,
the evidence of things not seen.

HEBREWS 11:1 NKJV

Faith is what makes the impossible possible. Our confidence that what we hope for will actually happen and our assurance about the things we cannot see stem from faith. Let this revelation comfort your worrying mind today!

# 1

# Rooted in Scripture

> These things I have written to you who believe
> in the name of the Son of God, that you may know
> that you have eternal life, and that you may continue
> to believe in the name of the Son of God.

1 JOHN 5:13 NKJV

We sometimes forget just how important scripture is to our faith—and just how amazing it is that we have scripture. In this passage from John's first epistle, we see that scripture, faith, and security are connected in a circle. Scripture is written for those who believe, but it only holds meaning in relation to the faith you bring to it. As your faith strengthens through reading scripture, you will feel more and more secure in the promise of eternity and unconditional love.

Let this truth inform the way you think, speak, and move on Earth. Combat negativity—whether from people in authority, loved ones, or yourself—with God's Word. Don't become a prisoner of your earthly mind; remember that your body may perish, but your soul will live on with God in Heaven! This month, be encouraged and challenge yourself to use the eternal truth of scripture to set you free.

Be diligent to present yourself approved to God,
a worker who does not need to be ashamed,
rightly dividing the word of truth.

2 TIMOTHY 2:15 NKJV

Your work, yourself, and anything that has your name attached to it should exude excellence. God rejoices when you apply the gifts He has given you toward a job well done, because you are a reflection of His greatness on Earth!

The Bible is the greatest of all books;
to study it is the noblest of all pursuits;
to understand it, the highest of all goals.

CHARLES C. RYRIE

Everything you need is in scripture. Make time to study the Bible this week and ask God to give you a discerning heart to help you understand what you read.

# 4

There is therefore now no condemnation
to those who are in Christ Jesus,
who do not walk according to the flesh,
but according to the Spirit.

ROMANS 8:1 NKJV

Honor the lifetime of grace you were given by God and choose to live by the Spirit. Don't let earthly pursuits dictate your life—walk in freedom today!

# 5

Looking away to Jesus each day,
Wonderful peace He brings to me;
Savior divine, I know He is mine,
Wonderful peace He brings to me.

"HE BRINGS ME PEACE" BY KATHRINE S. WADSWORTH

Seek Jesus each day. Not weekly, monthly, or yearly. Let Him lead you every day, and you will find peace.

For "whoever calls
on the name of the LORD
shall be saved."

ROMANS 10:13 NKJV

WHOEVER calls on Him is saved. God doesn't care about where you're coming from; if you call, He will answer, so let your faith rise to the occasion!

A new command I give you:
Love one another. As I have loved you,
so you must love one another.

JOHN 13:34 NIV

God's love can change someone's heart. How will you share God's love today?

## JULY

# 8

Is prayer your steering wheel
or your spare tire?

CORRIE TEN BOOM

Get back on course by saying this prayer today: "God,
forgive me for the arrogance of believing that I can live
life without prayer as my guidance. Help me get my pri-
orities together today, and release a fresh burning desire
in me to know you more. Amen."

## JULY

# 9

If you love Me,
keep My commandments.

JOHN 14:15 NKJV

Love isn't always easy or convenient. You need to put
in the work to keep it strong. Let your faith lead your
decisions as an act of worship to God.

For to us a child is born, to us a son is given,
and the government will be on his shoulders.
And he will be called Wonderful Counselor,
Mighty God, Everlasting Father, Prince of Peace.

ISAIAH 9:6 NIV

God is always God, and He is what you need when you
need it. If you need a friend, let Him be your friend. If
you need a parent, let Him be your parent. If you need
a role model, let Him be your role model. Let Him be who
He is so your strength can be renewed!

You are the light of the world.
A city that is set on a hill cannot be hidden.

MATTHEW 5:14 NKJV

As a believer, how are you shining light on your heavenly
Father for the world to see? Let your light shine today for
HIS glory!

# 12

Good work is giving to the poor and the helpless,
but divine work is showing them their
worth to the One who matters.

**CRISS JAMI**

All work is important, but it's definitely easier to invest
our money than to invest our time and energy. What can
you do—today, this week, this month, or this year—to
show someone that they are worthy of the perfect love
of Christ?

# 13

And you shall know the truth,
and the truth shall make you free.

**JOHN 8:32 NKJV**

Truth has the power to heal. Strengthening our faith
in eternal truth will make us free, and one way to
strengthen our faith is to be truthful with ourselves,
the world, and our God.

Anything under God's control
is never out of control.

CHARLES R. SWINDOLL

Sometimes it's hard to let go of control, but you will find freedom in uncertainty. Let your faith condition your mind to believe that everything will be okay because He loves you!

For the word of God is living and powerful,
and sharper than any two-edged sword, piercing even to
the division of soul and spirit, and of joints and marrow,
and is a discerner of the thoughts and intents of the heart.

HEBREWS 4:12 NKJV

The Word of God is meant to reach a place that only God can access. Your Creator wants to water the seed that He planted in you the moment you were born. Pray today for the Word to come alive in you in a new way!

# 16

I am standing on the Word of God, 'tis full of life divine;
God's Spirit lives in ev'ry word, and moves in ev'ry line.

"I AM STANDING ON THE WORD OF GOD"
BY E. M. WADSWORTH

The power of scripture never changes, but your relationship to scripture is always evolving. Ask God to reveal deeper levels of understanding, faith, and love in His living Word.

# 17

Confess your trespasses to one another,
and pray for one another, that you may be healed.
The effective, fervent prayer
of a righteous man avails much.

JAMES 5:16 NKJV

God wants you to open up to those you love and trust so that He can work through them to help you. Have faith and believe that healing is on the way.

Faith does not eliminate questions.
But faith knows where to take them.

ELISABETH ELLIOT

Having faith doesn't mean suppressing all of your doubts
or questions. Rather, having faith means working through
your doubts and questions with the Lord, who always
provides answers in His divine way, in His divine time.

I set My rainbow in the cloud,
and it shall be for the sign of the covenant
between Me and the earth.

GENESIS 9:13 NKJV

Are you open to the signs God is giving you? Don't
second-guess Him! Pray that God will give you a sign
that you need today and scripture to support it!

This man came for a witness,
to bear witness of the Light,
that all through him might believe.

JOHN 1:7 NKJV

God sent John the Baptist to announce that Jesus was coming to save the world. Who has God sent you to reveal His works in your life? Pray for discernment today!

Come unto me, when shadows darkly gather,
When the sad heart is weary and distrest,
Seeking for comfort from your Heavenly Father,
Come unto me, and I will give you rest!

"I WILL GIVE YOU REST" BY CATHERINE
HARBISON WATERMAN ESLING

Rest from the Lord is on a different level than the rest you get from sleeping, vacation, or venting. When your heart is heavy, He will provide the ultimate comfort.

Let this mind be in you
which was also in Christ Jesus.

PHILIPPIANS 2:5 NKJV

What have you been feeding your mind lately? Exercise
your mind with the Word of God so that you can take on
the world!

Jesus first, others next,
and yourself last spells J-O-Y.

LINDA BYLER

Prioritize selflessness with the strength of God's love!
Make J-O-Y your mantra!

The next day John saw Jesus coming toward
him, and said, "Behold! The Lamb of God
who takes away the sin of the world!"

JOHN 1:29 NKJV

John didn't hesitate when he saw Jesus. His strength of
faith allowed him to be completely confident. Ask God to
give you strength to act directly on your faith today!

Remember as you go about your day that you
may be the only Jesus some of your friends,
neighbors, and family will ever see.

WANDA E. BRUNSTETTER

Never forget how much your actions matter. As a
believer, you represent Christ every single day. Are
you making Him proud?

The earth was without form, and void;
and darkness was on the face of the deep.
And the Spirit of God was hovering
over the face of the waters.

GENESIS 1:2 NKJV

Don't be mistaken that our all-knowing God doesn't
understand darkness—He is at the root of creation. He
understands where you are in life right now. No matter
where you are, you are never alone.

If you measure your life by what you own,
the cavern of your heart will never be filled.

JAMES D. MAXON

God has placed eternity in our hearts so no tangible
asset will ever be able to fill the depths of your soul. Only
God can do that. Let your faith bring you peace today.

And I will pray the Father,
and He will give you another Helper,
that He may abide with you forever.

JOHN 14:16 NKJV

Jesus left the earth, but our Father gave us the Holy
Spirit to help see us through. Think of the Holy Spirit as
a 24/7, 365-day navigation system—with every move
you make, the Holy Spirit is recalculating your route.
The best part is that the destination never changes!

And you He made alive,
who were dead in trespasses and sins.

EPHESIANS 2:1 NKJV

You have already been granted eternal life—you have
grace for today and all your days to come. Show your
appreciation by vowing to renew your life daily.

God hears your every thought,
whether you dress it up with
"Thee" and "Thou" or not.

CATHERINE RICHMOND

You don't have to be polished when you go to God. He wants us to cry out like David in the Psalms! God accepts us no matter how vulnerable or raw we are, so be real with Him during your prayer time today and tell Him how you really feel.

The LORD is my Shepherd, I shall not want; In Him I now abide;
In pastures green He leadeth me, where quiet waters glide.
In mercy I cry, restore me again, give wisdom to my heart,
To choose the path of righteousness, and from it ne'er depart.

"HE LEADETH MY SOUL" BASED ON PSALM 23,
ARR. BY GRANT C. TULLAR

Your faith gives your soul a passport to transcend your body and enter into heavenly places. Meditate on His glory today and bask in His presence.

# 1

# Generosity

> He who has pity on the poor lends to the LORD,
> and He will pay back what he has given.

**PROVERBS 19:17 NKJV**

Giving is such a dynamic way to purify your heart. It goes beyond the contents of your wallet and even the walls of the church. Ministry extends into all areas of our lives, and generosity is an essential part of that ministry. As a believer, you are called to be generous!

The book of Proverbs is like a compilation of wisdom nuggets, and it's a great starting place to learn about how to act in the world. Generosity is about doing things that honor God's love in your heart without expecting something in return. In this scripture from Proverbs, Jesus says that when you're generous to others, you are also being generous to the Lord—that is a gift in and of itself. But the Lord will always pay back what you've given in one way or another.

Let this perspective encourage you to give more this month. When you give, don't do it because you will reap what you sow; do it because it's for God, and watch how your faith will rise!

God created everything through him,
and nothing was created except through him.

JOHN 1:3 NLT

Let your wandering mind find peace today with this
reminder: All things come from God—you are where
you need to be.

At thy heart the LORD is standing,
Griev'd and slighted o'er and o'er,
Still is knocking, pleading, calling,
Why not open now the door?

"JESUS AT THE DOOR" BY FANNY CROSBY

God will do anything for your love. He will call out to you,
grieve your absence, and wait for you patiently. Return
home today—He is waiting at the door of your heart!

4

And I also say to you that you are Peter,
and on this rock I will build My church,
and the gates of Hades shall not prevail against it.

MATTHEW 16:18 NKJV

God wants to use His sons and daughters to spread His
Word across the globe. You are a vessel that brings light
to the darkness, and like Peter, regardless of your sin,
mercy has enabled you to bring that light!

5

I have been crucified with Christ;
it is no longer I who live, but Christ lives in me;
and the life which I now live in the flesh
I live by faith in the Son of God,
who loved me and gave Himself for me.

GALATIANS 2:20 NKJV

Remind yourself today that it is not YOU who leads the
way, but God. He is alive in you, so let the Holy Spirit
lead you down the path to freedom. Trust that He is with
you, and let your faith rise.

6

Jesus, blessed Saviour, grant my earnest pray'r,
Take me now and keep me in Thy watchful care.
Keep me from the Tempter,
Shield me from his pow'r,
Whisper words of comfort in the trying hour.

"JESUS, BLESSED SAVIOR" BY FANNY CROSBY

Trying hours can be the most unbearable of all. But often our weakest moments allow us to become stronger than ever in our faith. Embrace the lessons pain offers, and watch your faith grow!

7

Do not think that I came to destroy the Law or the Prophets. I did not come to destroy but to fulfill.

MATTHEW 5:17 NKJV

Jesus came to fulfill—to make God's love known to us in the ultimate way. No matter what position you find yourself in today, remember that Jesus always fulfills our needs.

Always, everywhere God is present, and always
He seeks to discover Himself to each one.

A.W. TOZER

Even if you feel alone, search the depths of your soul to
find the still voice that says, "I am with you." Believe that
He is who He says He is!

So then faith comes by hearing,
and hearing by the word of God.

ROMANS 10:17 NKJV

To hear, we must listen without interruption, distrac-
tion, or projection. When we really listen to the Word of
God—when our minds are truly open to the meaning of
scripture—it is then that our faith is strengthened.

# 10

Dear Saviour! the battle of life is so great,
Its burdens for me are too heavy to bear;
I come, for with Thee it is never too late,
With faith and with confidence asking Thy care.

**"ASKING THY CARE" BY G.A. SANDERS**

You will not gain true peace from yoga, meditation, or attending a church service. Trying to fill an emotional void with a physical pleasure will lead you astray. Turn to the Creator of your soul. He will fill the void and bury the pain!

# 11

I am fallen, flawed, and imperfect.
Yet drenched in the grace and mercy that is
found in Jesus Christ, there is strength.

**ADAM YOUNG**

Sometimes when you fall, you lose your motivation to fight back. Today, standing or fallen, remember that your strength is found in the Creator. Through His grace, you are free from condemnation.

# 12

The Spirit of the LORD is on me,
because he has anointed me to proclaim good news
to the poor. He has sent me to proclaim freedom
for the prisoners and recovery of sight for
the blind, to set the oppressed free.

LUKE 4:18 NIV

Your life is a living testament to God's goodness. You
have the authority to speak your truth and share your
story. Challenge yourself to share the gospel today with
someone you don't know.

# 13

We may have done what the devil said we did,
but we are NOT who the devil says we are!

APRIL COFIELD ESSIX

Our past sins do NOT define who we are. They do not
make us inherently bad or unworthy of redemption. We
are already worthy because God says we are. Be free,
knowing that you have been redeemed and forgiven!

# 14

Everything may not be perfect.
There are things that may need to change,
but you have the grace to be happy today.

JOEL OSTEEN

Grace is a gift, and every single day you have the choice to accept it. Choose to accept what is freely given to you out of love, and let this gift bring you peace!

# 15

There's never a breath of your pray'r is lost,
You have His sweet promise true;
That there in the midst of His angel host,
The Savior remembers you.

"JESUS REMEMBERS YOU"
BY FRANCES MCKINNON MORTON

Not a single prayer goes unheard. He is with you when you suffer and when you rejoice. Let your faith lead you to believe that He will answer. Because He will.

## 16

However, when He, the Spirit of truth, has come,
He will guide you into all truth; for He will not speak
on His own authority, but whatever He hears He
will speak; and He will tell you things to come.

**JOHN 16:13 NKJV**

Today, pray that God gives you a better ear to hear His
guidance through the Holy Spirit, who will help you find
your way!

## 17

For Christ also suffered once for sins,
the just for the unjust,
that He might bring us to God,
being put to death in the flesh
but made alive by the Spirit.

**1 PETER 3:18 NKJV**

Jesus suffered so that we could be brought to God.
He bridged the gap for us, and now you, too, have the
power to bridge the gap of love in the world. Operate
with love so you can lead others to freedom.

It takes more courage to be humble
than it does to be prideful.

MATTHEW HAGEE

It's so easy to succumb to pride—it's what led to the
fall of humanity in Genesis, and it's still a natural human
instinct that we have to constantly fight against. Let your
faith lead you to humility, and trust that your courage will
be rewarded with peace.

Finally, my brethren,
be strong in the LORD
and in the power of His might.

EPHESIANS 6:10 NKJV

Strength requires work. Exercise your faith muscles
today by getting into the Word and feeding your soul
with truth!

# 20

Let every soul be subject to
the governing authorities.
For there is no authority except from God,
and the authorities that exist
are appointed by God.

**ROMANS 13:1 NKJV**

No matter what happens in politics around the world, remember that God always has the final say. He stands above all—look up to Him for leadership.

# 21

God is not confined by what you can imagine.

**LOUIE GIGLIO**

The older we get and the more challenging life becomes, the less imagination we can tap into. But even though we change, God always stays the same. Ask God to expand your imagination today.

# 22

He drove them all out of the temple,
with the sheep and the oxen, and poured out the
changers' money and overturned the tables.

JOHN 2:15 NKJV

When Jesus found that His Father's house was being used for selfish commercial interests, He became enraged. Learn from His anger—don't be complacent about things that are wrong in the world. Don't stand by when others disrespect the Lord. Channel the passion of Jesus!

# 23

Not all of us can do great things. But we
can do small things with great love.

MOTHER TERESA

It brings joy to God's heart when we are diligent in even the "small things" in life. No matter your status in the world, your sincere effort is what God sees.

## 24

He will wipe every tear from their eyes.
There will be no more death or mourning
or crying or pain, for the old order
of things has passed away.

REVELATION 21:4 NIV

This soothing comfort is promised in our eternal home in Heaven, but while we're here on Earth, the power dwells within us to choose hope over pain.

## 25

As it is written:
"There is none righteous, no, not one."

ROMANS 3:10 NKJV

The Word says that our righteousness is like a filthy rag. No one on Earth is perfect; we just have to keep cleansing our souls. Focus on keeping a clean heart today by purifying your intentions.

God is able to take the mess of our past and
turn it into a message. He takes the trials and
tests and turns them into a testimony.

CHRISTINE CAINE

God can make a masterpiece out of a mess—He is our
Creator, after all. Rest in His presence, knowing that
there is purpose in your pain.

But without faith it is impossible to please Him,
for he who comes to God must believe that He is,
and that He is a rewarder
of those who diligently seek Him.

HEBREWS 11:6 NKJV

Do you believe only what you can comprehend, or do
you believe because God is bigger than your circumstances? God is there waiting, but YOU must run to Him.

# 28

But the Helper, the Holy Spirit,
whom the Father will send in My name,
He will teach you all things, and bring to your
remembrance all things that I said to you.

JOHN 14:26 NKJV

The Holy Spirit is always present and ready to guide us, but sometimes He can't get through to us because our souls are so cluttered. Find some time to be still today, get past the clutter, and let the Spirit guide you to God.

# 29

Faith is believing BEFORE
what will only make sense AFTER.

STEVEN FURTICK

Faith doesn't always make sense at first, but you have to believe that God will never lead you astray. Ask Him to help open your heart today!

Most assuredly, I say to you, he who hears
My word and believes in Him who sent Me has
everlasting life, and shall not come into judgment,
but has passed from death into life.

JOHN 5:24 NKJV

God doesn't judge you—you're already forgiven. He
doesn't see your imperfections—He sees the blood of
Jesus. Praise God for sending His Son so that we could
walk in freedom!

Then God said, "Let the earth bring forth grass,
the herb that yields seed, and the fruit tree that
yields fruit according to its kind, whose seed
is in itself, on the earth"; and it was so.

GENESIS 1:11 NKJV

Use "and it was so" as a short but powerful anthem
to praise God today. Let these words remind you that
everything is from God, and when God speaks, everything WILL come to pass.

# 1

# Boldness

> And so, dear brothers and sisters,
> we can boldly enter heaven's Most Holy Place
> because of the blood of Jesus.

HEBREWS 10:19 NLT

Boldness is the willingness to take risks and act innovatively—having confidence or courage. As a believer, you should be bold in pursuing your life's purpose that God has created for you. If you're still not sure of your purpose, pray to God to show you! Our individual purposes may look different, but all believers share the greater purpose of being bold when proclaiming the gospel and spreading the light of Jesus in the world.

Fear is the greatest roadblock to being bold. But feeling fear isn't necessarily what makes us unable to be bold—it's the decision to let fear diminish our potential. The stronger we are in our faith, the easier it is for us to replace fear with God's love. To be bold, we must combat fear with faith! Motivate yourself to be bolder this month, knowing that God has called you to a greater purpose. Your destiny is waiting for you to arrive!

# 2

Prayer in private
results in boldness in public.

EDWIN LOUIS COLE

What's done in the dark will eventually come to light.
Strengthening your faith with quiet, internal reflection
will make you courageous to the world.

# 3

My brethren, count it all joy
when you fall into various trials.

JAMES 1:2 NKJV

It may seem difficult to feel joy during difficult times,
but God's Word reminds us that those are the moments
when our faith is most strengthened. Don't worry, He is
holding you!

# 4

He is the image of the invisible God,
the firstborn over all creation.

COLOSSIANS 1:15 NKJV

Faith is trusting God's leading even when you're blind-folded. God is still holding your hand as you walk the path He has laid out before you. Rest assured that He's divinely guiding you.

# 5

Just when I need Him, Jesus is near,
Just when I falter, just when I fear;
Ready to help me, ready to cheer,
Just when I need Him most.
Just when I need Him, Jesus is true,
Never forsaking, all the way through;
Giving for burdens pleasures anew,
Just when I need Him most.

"JUST WHEN I NEED HIM MOST" BY WILLIAM POOLE

God finds joy in our sorrows because that is when His glory has the opportunity to shine bright. Will you let His light shine through the darkness?

A man dies when he refuses to
stand up for that which is right.

MARTIN LUTHER KING JR.

Have you ever been too afraid to speak up, even though
you knew better? Next time remember that Jesus didn't
pay the wages of sin for us to be complacent! Let your
faith lead you to boldness so that you can shed light on
the darkness of the world.

Jesus said to him,
"You shall love the LORD your God with all your heart,
with all your soul, and with all your mind."

MATTHEW 22:37 NKJV

You can't fully love God with only a third of your
being. Even if you love God with your heart, you can't
fully love Him when you're distracted by negative
thoughts. Combat negativity with faith, and you will be
whole in God!

# 8

When you realize that God loves you
and that He has a plan for your life,
you can walk with your head held high–totally
confident in who He created you to be.

JOYCE MEYER

Confidence comes from God, not us. When your faith is strong, you can finally feel confident in His purpose for you. Pray for Him to guide you!

# 9

The light shines in the darkness,
and the darkness can never extinguish it.

JOHN 1:5 NLT

Once the light of God touches your heart, the darkness cannot overcome it again. This does not mean that you won't experience pain ever again, but the pain will never defeat you!

Jesus knows all about the pathway
I must travel from day to day,
When on earth as a "Man of Sorrows,"
He walked over the same hard way.

"KEPT THROUGH FAITH" BY CIVILLA D. MARTIN

Jesus knows what it's like to struggle on Earth. Know that He is right there with you. There is nothing in this world, big or small, that you can't overcome with Jesus on your side.

He has shown you, O man, what is good;
and what does the Lord require of you
but to do justly, to love mercy, and to
walk humbly with your God?

MICAH 6:8 NKJV

God doesn't demand superficial praise or gifts. He demands that we be the best we can be—to do what is right through His perfect love and keep trying even when we falter.

Refuse to be average.
Let your heart soar as high as it will.

A.W. TOZER

God has given every single person a divine and specific calling on their life. Your journey of faith will lead your heart to where it uniquely belongs. Let your faith be your means to freedom!

Sanctify them by Your truth.
Your word is truth.

JOHN 17:17 NKJV

God has set you apart from the world. You are walking on Earth but always protected by His blessing. Let that truth prop you up today as you maneuver through the world.

# 14

So they said,
"Believe on the LORD Jesus Christ,
and you will be saved,
you and your household."

ACTS 16:31 NKJV

This verse is a reminder not just to believe for yourself but also for your loved ones and the rest of the world. Pray that they may find truth and salvation in their own journeys.

# 15

Stop worrying about what you aren't and
start being happy about who you are.

JOHN HAGEE

God didn't make any two people exactly the same. Even twins have different souls! Embrace your differences today because God made you on purpose.

Jesus said to her,
"I am the resurrection and the life.
He who believes in Me,
though he may die, he shall live."

**JOHN 11:25 NKJV**

You've already overcome the ultimate fear—death. Your body may perish, but your soul will live forever with the Lord in Heaven! Take courage in this truth today!

Jesus said to them, "Most assuredly, I say
to you, before Abraham was, I AM."

**JOHN 8:58 NKJV**

The people were arguing with Jesus because they didn't believe His motives or who He claimed to be. But in this verse Jesus asserts "I AM." He is our rock, unchanging in the past, present, or future!

# 18

There's a land of light
Where there is no night,
And sorrow and sin come never,
Where the angels raise
Loudest songs of praise
To God and the Lamb forever.

**"LAND OF LIGHT" BY WILLIAM STEVENSON**

Our reunion with God in Heaven is what our life is all about. It's more meaningful than any salary, any amount of Instagram followers, or any prize on Earth. Let this vision inspire you today in your actions!

# 19

Train up a child in the way he should go,
And when he is old he will not depart from it.

**PROVERBS 22:6 NKJV**

Even though we get older, we're all still children of God, continually developing our faith in Him. Train yourself up in the Word of God so that when hard times come around, you will not depart from it!

# 20

Sometimes what makes us insecure and vulnerable
becomes the fuel we need to be overachievers.
The antidote for a snakebite is made from the
poison, and the thing that made you go backward
is the same force that will push you forward.

T.D. JAKES

God will test you by using the very thing you think is
going to kill you—to prove that it can't. He is pushing
you toward your purpose. Lean into the struggle. Healing
is on the way.

# 21

And [the serpent] said to the woman,
"Has God indeed said, 'You shall not eat
of every tree of the garden'?"

GENESIS 3:1 NKJV

The evil one will try to plant doubt in your mind and use
tricks to throw you off course. Combat that voice of fear
by standing firm on God's Word.

Faith doesn't always mean that
God changes your situation.
Sometimes it means He changes you.

STEVEN FURTICK

God is in the heart surgery business—not the plastic
surgery business! He will always give you what you need,
but that doesn't mean money or love potions. He wants
you to find true freedom through faith.

If any of you lacks wisdom, let him ask of God,
who gives to all liberally and without
reproach, and it will be given to him.

JAMES 1:5 NKJV

Asking God to give you wisdom, or anything else, means
being open to letting Him place you in a situation where
you'll have to learn by trial. Trust that your faith will give
you the discernment to understand the lesson.

There are far, far better things ahead
than any we leave behind.

C.S. LEWIS

Maybe life is going really well, and the idea of that
changing is scary. Know that no matter how perfect
things may be, the promise of eternal life is the most
comforting future of all.

God, who at various times and in various ways spoke in
time past to the fathers by the prophets, has in these last
days spoken to us by His Son, whom He has appointed heir
of all things, through whom also He made the worlds.

HEBREWS 1:1-2 NKJV

God speaks to us in many ways. Pray for a discerning ear
to hear His voice today!

Guide my footsteps, Father, lead me lest I stray;
Let Thy hand unerring point out all my way.
When the road is dreary, and my soul is sad,
When my heart is weary, do Thou make me glad.

"LEAD ME" BY LOUISE F. EMANUEL

Things can get so messy that sometimes the only comfort you have is knowing that God is with you. Guess what? That is enough to keep going!

Behold, I stand at the door and knock. If anyone
hears My voice and opens the door, I will come in
to him and dine with him, and he with Me.

REVELATION 3:20 NKJV

God invites us to open the door; He doesn't force His way into our lives. Today, ask God to open your ears and heart so you can respond to His knock. If the door's already open, He could be knocking so that you'll invite someone else into the family of true love!

Instead of judging people, why don't you take that
same time to pray for them, to reach out to them,
to let them know that you believe in them.

JOEL OSTEEN

BE the change you want to see in the world through
God's love and light! Jesus demonstrated that kindness
can achieve powerful results, so go out of your way to
extend grace to all.

But sanctify the LORD God in your hearts,
and always be ready to give a defense to
everyone who asks you a reason for the hope that
is in you, with meekness and fear.

1 PETER 3:15 NKJV

How do you express your relationship with God to others?
Remember that the strength of your private faith will give
you boldness to share God's love in public. Is your faith
your way of life?

30

True humility is not thinking less of yourself;
it is thinking of yourself less.

RICK WARREN

Negative self-talk is also a form of pride. You are already
worthy because God says you are, so why are you
questioning Him? Look beyond yourself to see the bigger
picture God has given you!

# 1

# Discipline

Whoever loves discipline loves knowledge,
but whoever hates correction is stupid.

PROVERBS 12:1 NIV

Discipline is a tool we need to become better at something, whether it's being more productive at work, exercising to be healthy, or being a better friend. But some people want to improve themselves just for the sake of being better than others—missing the point entirely! Discipline is meant to teach us self-restraint, not self-righteousness. If you can't accept it when others correct you, your mind is too filled with pride to be open to God.

So how do we realign our intentions? Start by prioritizing the area of your life that deserves the most discipline—your faith. God wants to pour His wisdom into your heart, but it takes daily work to be able to truly surrender and fully open up to Him. Are you putting in the work? Are you able to hear God when He is trying to correct you? This month, strengthen your discipline of faith so that you can better follow God!

The LORD had said to Abram, "Go from your country, your people and your father's household to the land I will show you."

GENESIS 12:1 NIV

It's scary to make big life changes like moving, starting a business, or saying yes—or no—to a new opportunity. But if you listen to God, He will not leave your side. Have faith to take a risk even if you're not yet sure how it will work out.

Jesus, let me cling to thee, show thy mercy now to me;
I am lonely, weak, oppressed; I am weary, give me rest.
Should I wander from thy side, Thou, my ever-faithful guide,
Wilt restore me to the right, and in darkness grant me light.

"LET ME CLING TO THEE" BY FANNY CROSBY

Cling to the hem of the Lord's garment as tightly as you can—in darkness, you will never stray too far from the light of Jesus.

And the Lord God formed man of the dust of the
ground, and breathed into his nostrils the breath
of life; and man became a living being.

GENESIS 2:7 NKJV

God's breath flows through each and every one of us. Be
mindful of your breath today and feel the strength of the
Lord in it. God gave us life, and thus the power to create,
love, and make a difference in the world. Let your faith
rise to meet your breath!

Forgiveness is an act of the will,
and the will can function regardless of
the temperature of the heart.

CORRIE TEN BOOM

Check your heart's posture today. Are you letting the
principles of your faith inform the emotions of your
heart, or vice versa? Emotions change like the wind,
but the principles of your faith are a firm foundation!

Keep your lives free from the love of money
and be content with what you have,
because God has said, "Never will I leave
you; never will I forsake you."

HEBREWS 13:5 NIV

Reevaluate your attachment to possessions. If everything
were taken away, would you still be satisfied with only
God's love? If the possibility of losing everything makes
you fearful, you've got some work to do!

Dear friends, do not believe every spirit,
but test the spirits to see whether they are
from God, because many false prophets
have gone out into the world.

1 JOHN 4:1 NIV

Every sign or voice is not from God. Sometimes the false
prophet is our own voice getting in the way. Pray and ask
God for clarity and have faith that He will answer you.

8

God allows us to experience the low points of life
in order to teach us lessons that
we could learn in no other way.

C.S. LEWIS

God doesn't waste anything or any moment. Sometimes
you have to go down to come up again, but your heart
will be lighter than before. Be grateful for the strength
you gain in the process!

9

Every good gift and every perfect gift is from above,
and comes down from the Father of lights, with
whom there is no variation or shadow of turning.

JAMES 1:17 NKJV

You don't have to doubt God's gifts. There is no trickery
from Him, just perfect love. Believe that whatever He
says is good really is.

Do not lay up for yourselves treasures on earth, where moth and rust destroy and where thieves break in and steal; but lay up for yourselves treasures in heaven, where neither moth nor rust destroys and where thieves do not break in and steal.

MATTHEW 6:19-20 NKJV

True treasures are intangible. Treasures like love, humility, and selflessness are stored in Heaven and are worth more than anything on Earth.

Never be afraid to trust an unknown future to a known God.

CORRIE TEN BOOM

All you have to know is that God commands everything. Let go of the unknown—God orchestrates all things to work together for your good!

# 12

Act, and God will act.

**JOAN OF ARC**

Challenge yourself to make a move today, trusting that God is already ahead of you. Act on your faith and demonstrate your trust in Him!

# 13

On a firm foundation let us build our hopes,
And not on the drifting sand;
For the tempest's shock will surely come at last;
Then how can we safely stand?
On the Rock of Ages let us strongly build,
The Rock that is steadfast, sure;
On a firm foundation that no storm can shake,
That will to the end endure.

**"LET US BUILD ON THE ROCK" BY FRANK M. DAVIS**

No one is exempt from temptation, but as a believer, your faith will keep you steady and act as a shield for your soul. Faith is true freedom!

Is anyone among you sick? Let him call for the elders of the church, and let them pray over him, anointing him with oil in the name of the LORD.

JAMES 5:14 NKJV

Who is there for you in times of spiritual need? Who are you there for in times of spiritual need? A strong community makes us grow stronger in Christ. Pray to find believers that will be there when you need them.

For we do not wrestle against flesh and blood, but against principalities, against powers, against the rulers of the darkness of this age, against spiritual hosts of wickedness in the heavenly places.

EPHESIANS 6:12 NKJV

Life sometimes feels like a physical battle, but the real war is spiritual. Eternity with God is more real than the world you see with your eyes. Remember this truth in difficult times.

# 16

By love never failing, love gentle and kind,
Love showing forth daily the Master's own mind,
By love that in serving new blessings will find,
Let others see Jesus in you.

"LET OTHERS SEE JESUS IN YOU" BY ELIZA E. HEWITT

When you give love to others, you are showing them what it means to be loved by a perfect God. Don't be stingy with the goodness of God—shine your light warmly on those in need!

# 17

Repent therefore and be converted, that your sins may be blotted out, so that times of refreshing may come from the presence of the LORD.

ACTS 3:19 NKJV

Repenting doesn't just mean asking for forgiveness and continuing to sin; it means constantly making the effort to be better. We should ask the Lord to help us break bad habits and make better choices in His name daily.

For we are His workmanship,
created in Christ Jesus for good works,
which God prepared beforehand
that we should walk in them.

EPHESIANS 2:10 NKJV

You were created for specific works that only YOU will accomplish in this world. He prepared you before you were even born, so don't think you aren't fully equipped to fulfill your potential. Let your faith lead the way!

A setback is a setup for a comeback.

T.D. JAKES

Setbacks make it possible for our faith to transform our hearts and minds completely so that we can keep purifying ourselves and getting closer to God's purpose for us. Hold on—your new future is closer than you think!

# 20

What shall we say then?
Shall we continue in sin
that grace may abound?

ROMANS 6:1 NKJV

Grace is a gift, and when we abuse it or use grace as an excuse to sin, we get stuck in a cycle of failure. Remember that grace is intended to help you to "fail forward" and move on from your mistakes.

# 21

Success is on the same road as failure;
success is just a little further down the road.

JACK HYLES

The journey of faith isn't always a straight shot, and as a believer, you've got to have grit for the ride. But always remember that no matter how many bumps and detours lie ahead, the destination at the end of the road is worth it.

Moreover, if your brother sins against you,
go and tell him his fault between you and him alone.
If he hears you, you have gained your brother.

MATTHEW 18:15 NKJV

Not all confrontation is bad. Proverbs 27:17 NKJV tells us "iron sharpens iron." We need to give people the opportunity to change—and we need them to show us our blind spots as well. Be open in both ways today.

Focusing on God's promises
instead of the world's problems is the
best way to overcome fear.

JOYCE MEYER

The problems of the world can be overwhelming and hard to escape. Write down God's promise for your life on a sticky note today and read it every hour. Your faith will rise.

# 24

They are of the world.
Therefore, they speak as of the world, and the world hears
them. We are of God. He who knows God hears us;
he who is not of God does not hear us. By this we
know the spirit of truth and the spirit of error.

1 JOHN 4:5-6

As believers, we have access to divine truth, which
makes it possible for us to shut off the noise of Earth and
focus on the freedom of Heaven. Share the hopeful joy
that your faith has granted you. Be a light!

# 25

I have told you these things, so that in me you may
have peace. In this world you will have trouble.
But take heart! I have overcome the world.

JOHN 16:33 NIV

Let your hope rise even in troubled times, because you
serve a God who has overcome every battle you will face
in your lifetime. Claim your soul's peace in Jesus's name!

# 26

Love divine, all loves excelling, Joy of heav'n to earth come down;
Fix in us Thy humble dwelling; All Thy faithful mercies crown:
Jesus, Thou art all compassion, Pure unbounded love Thou art;
Visit us with Thy salvation; Enter every trembling heart.

"LOVE DIVINE, ALL LOVES EXCELLING"
BY CHARLES WESLEY

God came down from Heaven just to be near you on Earth. Today, let your faith lead you back to His heavenly home and His blissful presence.

🙠

# 27

The LORD is not slack concerning His promise,
as some count slackness, but is longsuffering
toward us, not willing that any should perish
but that all should come to repentance.

2 PETER 3:9 NKJV

There is meaning in seasons of waiting. God not only wants to do more work in your heart but also in the hearts of all, and He may require your help. Today, pray for understanding instead of a speedy miracle.

# 28

Do not judge,
or you too will be judged.

**MATTHEW 7:1 NIV**

If you sow negativity, you will reap negativity. But if
you sow love, you will receive love. Let this simple truth
change the trajectory of your day.

# 29

In prayer you gain your strength–the power
to gird yourself with armor that extinguishes
every weapon your enemy wields.

**PRISCILLA SHIRER**

How do you fight your battles? Instead of venting to
a friend or loved one today, try going to the One who
already knows what you need. Faith will cast out fear
and give you courage.

Then Jesus was led up by the Spirit
into the wilderness to be tempted by the devil.

MATTHEW 4:1 NKJV

You will not bear any temptation that you cannot handle.
God is not an overbearing God, but He will push your
limits to show you that you are stronger than you think.
Use your faith to persevere!

Cruelty and wrong are not the greatest forces
in the world. There is nothing eternal
in them. Only love is eternal.

ELISABETH ELLIOT

Many people mask their pain with cruelty, all because
they're actually longing for a deep sense of love and
acceptance. As a believer, you know the power of God's
eternal love. Today, help someone else take the mask off.

# 1

# Thankfulness

> Oh, give thanks to the LORD, for He is good!
> For His mercy endures forever.

**PSALM 107:1 NKJV**

It's the holiday season, which evokes a lot of emotions—joy, stress, loneliness, peace. Whether you love this time of year or find it difficult, take a step back, notice how you feel, and evaluate where your heart is. It's imperative to your faith that you keep a pure heart for yourself and others around you, especially during this time.

The enemy wants to steal, kill, and destroy our faith, and one way he tries to do that is by manipulating your hope to try to make your heart cold. As you head into the holiday season, you can keep your heart warm and pure by remembering one thing above all—thankfulness. It's referenced often, especially in November, but remember that thankfulness isn't just about giving thanks for the superficial things you have, like gifts and food. Let this Psalm remind you that giving thanks to God for His mercy means showing mercy to those around you. Be thankful this season and give whatever you can to those who are in need.

No one has ever seen God. But the unique One, who is himself God, is near to the Father's heart. He has revealed God to us.

JOHN 1:18 NLT

Isn't it beautiful that God sent Jesus just so we could be near Him? God met you right where you are instead of requiring you to reach out to Him. Let this truth fill your heart with love today.

More living faith, O Saviour,
We daily, hourly need,
That we may come with boldness,
For dying souls to plead.
More earnest faith to labor,
More ardent faith to pray,
More steadfast faith to follow
Where Thou dost lead the way.

"MORE FAITH IN THEE" BY FANNY CROSBY

The moment you realize that you need the Savior every second of the day will be the moment you find true strength in your faith. Let Him lead you to still waters today!

4

I, therefore, the prisoner of the LORD,
beseech you to walk worthy of the calling
with which you were called.

EPHESIANS 4:1 NKJV

Live a life worthy of the calling you have received. You were uniquely created to achieve something only you can. Today, ask God to reveal His plan for you and to give you the courage to chase after it relentlessly.

5

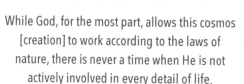

While God, for the most part, allows this cosmos
[creation] to work according to the laws of
nature, there is never a time when He is not
actively involved in every detail of life.

CHARLES R. SWINDOLL

God didn't sign off after creating the world—He is present everywhere, at all times, and His spiritual rule commands all physical law. Appreciate God in nature today and give thanks for His beautiful creation.

6

And do not be drunk with wine, in which is
dissipation; but be filled with the Spirit.

EPHESIANS 5:18 NKJV

As humans prone to error, we turn to coping mechanisms like alcohol or binge eating during difficult times. Instead of filling yourself with things that make you feel bad, fill yourself with the Word of God for comfort. You'll be more satisfied than you've ever been!

7

Every adversity brings
new experiences and new lessons.

LAILAH GIFTY AKITA

Every high and every low is meant to mold your heart into the person you were designed to be. The lessons you learn along the way will help you find relief from your pain.

NOVEMBER

8

Now I saw a new heaven and a new earth, for the first heaven and the first earth had passed away. Also there was no more sea.

REVELATION 21:1 NKJV

All things are made new in God's perfect time. Have faith and believe that no matter the difficulties with which you may be struggling, this too shall pass.

NOVEMBER

9

God knew He had to create you in a way that would suit your story.

TESSA EMILY HALL

Every aspect of who you are is on purpose. God knew what He was doing when He made you, and He loves you perfectly. Your beauty shines when you come to love yourself for who God made you to be!

# 10

But you, Bethlehem Ephrathah, though you are little among the thousands of Judah, yet out of you shall come forth to Me the One to be Ruler in Israel, whose goings forth are from of old, from everlasting.

MICAH 5:2 NKJV

Don't despise small beginnings. You might not feel like your purpose in the world is being realized, but God has a reason for everything. Instead of asking God to hurry, ask Him to prepare you for what's to come during this season of waiting. Great things are ahead for you!

# 11

Then, the same day at evening, being the first day of the week, when the doors were shut where the disciples were assembled, for fear of the Jews, Jesus came and stood in the midst, and said to them, "Peace be with you."

JOHN 20:19 NKJV

God declared peace in your soul the moment you put your faith in Him. Shut the door to the world today so you can hear His voice declaring His perfect love for you.

# 12

My God, how endless is Thy love!
Thy gifts are every evening new;
And morning mercies from above
Gently distill like early dew.

"MY GOD, HOW ENDLESS IS THY LOVE"
BY ISAAC WATTS

His love is never-ending—no matter how far you go astray, you're never out of His reach!

# 13

MOVE—it's what Jesus did!

PASTOR CARLOS TORRES

Scripture shows us that Jesus was still only when He went into isolation to pray. He constantly moved from place to place, teaching people the truth that would set them free. God didn't call you to be stagnant—be like Jesus and get moving!

In Him we have redemption through His blood,
the forgiveness of sins,
according to the riches of His grace.

EPHESIANS 1:7 NKJV

You are redeemed because Jesus died for you. Your sins are forgiven, and they will always be forgiven if you repent. All of this mercy is by the grace of God—let this revelation fill you with thankfulness today!

When you understand that life is a test,
you realize that nothing
is insignificant in your life.

RICK WARREN

The Word says to do everything as if you are doing it for the Lord Himself. Don't take any moment for granted today—feel empowered in everything you do, no matter how small.

But if we walk in the light as He is in the light,
we have fellowship with one another,
and the blood of Jesus Christ
His Son cleanses us from all sin.

1 JOHN 1:7 NKJV

Walking in the light does not mean walking in perfection; it means walking in the grace of God and receiving His gift of forgiveness through our faith. Feel free knowing that you are forgiven!

And the LORD God said,
"It is not good that man should be alone;
I will make him a helper comparable to him."

GENESIS 2:18 NKJV

You may read verses like this one and think, "If God intervened to give Adam the help he needed, why won't He do that for me?" The answer is that God has already given you everything you need, right inside of you. Believe in yourself and unlock your faith.

Christ literally walked in our shoes.

TIMOTHY J. KELLER

There is no pain that you have endured that Jesus doesn't know. He loved you enough to endure the ultimate pain and win the battle for you. Let that truth fill your heart with love today.

But you are not in the flesh but in the Spirit,
if indeed the Spirit of God dwells in you.
Now if anyone does not have
the Spirit of Christ, he is not His.

ROMANS 8:9 NKJV

Because the Spirit of God lives in you, you are in the realm of the Spirit and not the flesh. As you fight life's battles today, remember that what you bind in Heaven will be bound on Earth. The way to win is through prayer!

My Saviour is with me, wherever I go,
In darkness and danger the way He doth show;
When storms rage around me, and sorrows increase,
He stilleth the tempest and giveth me peace.

**"MY SAVIOUR IS WITH ME" BY ADA BLENKHORN**

When God speaks, Heaven and Earth shift. His Word has the same power to move mountains in your life. Remember that He's with you every step of the way.

I say then: Walk in the Spirit, and you shall
not fulfill the lust of the flesh.

**GALATIANS 5:16 NKJV**

Because we live on Earth, temptations are present every day of our lives. But remember that the Holy Spirit resides within you. If you fill your heart with the Word of God daily, you will be able to overcome base desires that lead to bad decisions. Discipline yourself to seek the Lord in prayer when you're being tempted!

Take the limits off of yourself.
You will never rise higher than your thinking.
Create a great vision for your life.

JOEL OSTEEN

We often self-sabotage by limiting our potential. If
you've already been given a vision for your life, ask God
to give you the resilience to realize it. If you don't have
a vision for your life yet, ask God to make His vision
clear to you!

And as Moses lifted up the serpent in the wilderness,
even so must the Son of Man be lifted up.

JOHN 3:14 NKJV

In this verse Jesus is foreshadowing His own execution
on the cross. Knowing He made such a great sacrifice to
save you, let His pure love inspire your heart, and lift Him
up rightfully today.

The greater your knowledge of the goodness
and grace of God on your life, the more likely
you are to praise Him in the storm.

MATT CHANDLER

It takes strength to realize that sometimes storms come
into our lives to break things that we don't have the
discipline to break on our own. Will you trust God's
sovereignty or keep leading your own life?

Enter by the narrow gate; for wide is the gate
and broad is the way that leads to destruction,
and there are many who go in by it.

MATTHEW 7:13 NKJV

Think of the narrow gate as living God's way and the
broad gate as living the world's way. No one said that
the narrow gate would be easier, but it yields a whole-
ness that the broad gate can never offer. Let your faith
lead you!

Your potential is the sum of all the
possibilities God has for your life.

CHARLES STANLEY

The caveat to this revelation is that you must decide
what you will do with that potential. God has gifted you
with certain skills so that you can use them to change
the world. Don't sleep on your talents!

Nearer the cross of Jesus
Ever let me be;
Nearer the flowing fountain,
That cleanseth me.
Nearer the cross of Jesus
There I would abide;
There let me rest forever,
Near Jesus' side.

"NEARER THE CROSS" BY CHARLOTTE ABBEY

Hold God's hand today as you walk the earth. Let His
spirit guide you into the unknown. Let your hope rise,
because there is nothing sweeter than being by His side!

# 28

But be doers of the word,
and not hearers only, deceiving yourselves.

JAMES 1:22 NKJV

God doesn't want us to be greedy. Don't just fill yourself
up with the Word and sit on it. Take the Word and put it
to work! Remember that you might offer the opportunity
for someone else to witness the light of Jesus.

# 29

Don't let the devil shut your mouth;
this is the season to declare your deliverance.
Take authority over your atmosphere.

REAL TALK KIM

The moment you put your faith in Jesus was the moment
you were granted the power to claim authority over your
atmosphere through His guidance. If things are tense,
declare peace. If there is pain, declare healing. If there is
worry, declare your faith!

30

My sheep hear My voice,
and I know them, and they follow Me.

JOHN 10:27 NKJV

When you hear God's voice, do you follow Him or hesitate? Your ability to act when you hear the voice of God has the potential to unlock your blessings! Let your faith be the catalyst of your action!

# 1

## Secure in Jesus

The LORD is my light and my salvation; whom shall I fear?
The LORD is the strength of my life; of whom shall I be afraid?
The LORD is my light and my salvation; whom shall I fear? The
LORD is the strength of my life; of whom shall I be afraid?

PSALM 27:1-2 NKJV

As the year comes to an end, new beginnings come to mind. Jesus
was born to give us all a new beginning through eternal salvation.
So why do we still have fear?

The enemy uses fear to deter us from our faith, even pitting our
own voice against us with negative self-talk. But your doubts are no
match for HIS perfect love. Even when you stray, He is waiting with
open arms. You can ALWAYS go back to Him.

Take this month to reflect on the past year. Have you strayed or
strengthened your faith? Either way, take this season to renew your
trust in God's love. End the year at peace with this truth: "The Lord
is the strength of my life."

For by Him all things were created that are in heaven
and that are on earth, visible and invisible, whether
thrones or dominions or principalities or powers. All
things were created through Him and for Him.

COLOSSIANS 1:16 NKJV

ALL things were created for God's glory—including
your success. Don't get caught up in all that you have
achieved without giving God the glory for bringing you
to that success!

## 3

Nothing will work unless you do.

MAYA ANGELOU

This truth applies to studying scripture, too. Just
because you read the Word doesn't mean it will make
itself evident to you. You have to invest time and energy
daily in your faith and Bible studies to see change!

# 4

If then you were raised with Christ,
seek those things which are above, where
Christ is, sitting at the right hand of God.

COLOSSIANS 3:1 NKJV

What are you seeking to gain through your faith? Are
you seeking superficial rewards like money, influence,
and power? Challenge yourself to actively seek peace,
hope, love, and grace.

# 5

Nevertheless, I tell you the truth. It is to your advantage
that I go away; for if I do not go away, the Helper will not
come to you; but if I depart, I will send Him to you.

JOHN 16:7 NKJV

Even though Jesus went to be with His Father in Heaven,
He didn't leave us alone. In fact, His departure allowed
the Holy Spirit to enter us all. Rest today, knowing that it
is within you and that He will not lead you astray.

In the day of trial, in the hour of need,
I have found a friend indeed;
Yes, a faithful friend, whom I have often tried,
Jesus who was crucified.

"A FRIEND INDEED" BY J.B. MACKAY

During trying times, God is with you. In Christ you have a friend who will sit with you no matter how difficult the circumstances. Rely on Him as your source of comfort and peace.

For the grace of God that brings salvation
has appeared to all men.

TITUS 2:11 NKJV

Without grace there would be no salvation. You are saved and secure because Jesus paid the cost for you. Don't be afraid, have hope, and know that His perfect love will cover you forever.

The weak can never forgive.
Forgiveness is the attribute of the strong.

MAHATMA GANDHI

Instead of thinking about the offender when it comes to forgiveness, think about what Jesus did for you and your sins. Let your faith guide you to the freedom of forgiveness before the year is out.

For everyone who asks receives,
and he who seeks finds,
and to him who knocks it will be opened.

MATTHEW 7:8 NKJV

God already knows what you need, but He wants you to ask for it. Are you taking the initiative or being passive in your pursuit of freedom?

You are the salt of the earth;
but if the salt loses its flavor, how shall it be
seasoned? It is then good for nothing but to be
thrown out and trampled underfoot by men.

MATTHEW 5:13 NKJV

Consider the flavor of your faith. If you don't practice
your faith and remain close to God, you will become
distant from Him and lose your ability to spread His love.
Let your faith make you salty!

Precious love that gives me proof,
Whatever may betide me.
Jesus gave His life to save,
And He will safely hide me.

"SAFELY HIDE ME" BY JOHN H. KURZENKNABE

Your refuge can be found in Jesus because of His great
sacrifice. If you are worried today, rest in His sweet
hiding place.

## 12

Dreams are free. When one dream falls apart,
you have to have enough courage
to dream a new dream.

EARLENE BUGGS

Remember that dreams come from God, and when one of our aspirations isn't realized, it wasn't meant to be. Having enough courage to dream a new dream means having enough faith to trust in God's plan for your life.

Therefore, submit to God.
Resist the devil and he will flee from you.

JAMES 4:7 NKJV

This verse reveals that temptation comes even after we submit ourselves to God. Putting your faith in God does not mean you are free from the weapons against you (Isaiah 54:17 NKJV). It just means that none of them will prosper!

The truth is that past mistakes and disappointments
are the elements you need to reframe your
mind, refine your vision, and boost an attitude
of resilience for future achievements.

ILKA TORRES MURRAY

Everything in your life has been planned by God. Instead
of letting the pain and frustration of your past drag you
down, use all of your experiences as tools to make you
a better person for tomorrow!

I am the good shepherd.
The good shepherd gives His life for the sheep.

JOHN 10:11 NKJV

The Lamb of God was the sacrifice that ensured our
freedom. Celebrate this profound truth and be glad that
you have the key to eternal life!

# 16

'Tis a blessed hope, and it cheers my soul,
That I shall rest, sweetly rest, by and by.
When my work is done and my crown is won,
Then I shall rest, sweetly rest, by and by.

"REST OVER JORDAN" BY FANNY CROSBY

Don't mistake the sweet rest God offers for an excuse to be lazy. He only blesses your faith with action. Get up and move today and let your faith lead you!

# 17

Who Himself bore our sins in His own body
on the tree, that we, having died to sins,
might live for righteousness—by whose
stripes you were healed.

1 PETER 2:24 NKJV

Never forget the pain Jesus endured to bear our shame of sin. Never take for granted what He gave us—the greatest gift of all, the ability to go back to the Lord.

We have tricked ourselves into incredible smallness,
engaging in a fight with our own blindness, not people.
Once we awaken to this, we must be fearless enough
to give ourselves the love that we didn't receive.

FELECIA HENDERSON

Are you using the trials of the world as an excuse for
your negative self-talk? Check yourself today and ask
God to show you what unfiltered faith looks like.

All that the Father gives Me will come to Me,
and the one who comes to Me
I will by no means cast out.

JOHN 6:37 NKJV

Accepting that what you're hoping for will only be
given when God says the time is right requires extreme
patience. If you find yourself worrying or growing anxious, go to Him so that He can still your heart.

# 20

Likewise, the Spirit also helps in our weaknesses.
For we do not know what we should pray for as we
ought, but the Spirit Himself makes intercession
for us with groanings which cannot be uttered.

ROMANS 8:26 NKJV

Isn't it amazing that even if we don't know what to say in prayer, God can still interpret our cries through the Holy Spirit within us? Take a moment to praise Him today for being a God who can recognize exactly what we need through our frail prayers.

DECEMBER

# 21

Just because things are not going the way
you want them to, does not mean
things are not going your way.

DEWAYNE OWENS

True faith sees the silver lining in the black cloud. Do you trust God with your life even if it doesn't seem like life is going your way?

Now the first day of the week Mary Magdalene
went to the tomb early, while it was still dark,
and saw that the stone had been
taken away from the tomb.

JOHN 20:1 NKJV

God will answer your prayers in unexpected ways. Mary Magdalene went to the tomb expecting to find Jesus— but the stone was gone, and Jesus had risen. Don't be afraid of the unexpected!

Then Jesus answered and said to them,
"Most assuredly, I say to you,
the Son can do nothing of Himself, but what
He sees the Father do; for whatever He does,
the Son also does in like manner."

JOHN 5:19 NKJV

Jesus was with God and God was with Him. Because of your faith, God is also within you, guiding you every step of the way.

## 24

There are only two kinds of people:
those who say to God, "Thy will be done,"
and those to whom God says,
"All right, then, have it your way."

C.S. LEWIS

What kind of person are you? You have seven days left
to renew your faith in God before the year's end. Have
faith to let go of control!

## 25

The virgin will conceive and give birth to
a son, and they will call him Immanuel.

MATTHEW 1:23 NIV

Even before Jesus was born, He was destined to be
with us until the end of time. Sing out "Immanuel" today!
Rejoice in the happiest of celebrations, the birth of
Jesus, by renewing your faith!

Do not love the world or the things in the world.
If anyone loves the world,
the love of the Father is not in him.

1 JOHN 2:15 NKJV

Do you have enough room in your heart to love God?
Or are you consumed with your love of worldly things?
Let your faith lead you instead of your flesh.

Where spend eternity
When earth is gone?
Where will my spirit be as time goes on?
Earth's pleasures cannot stay,
Soon, soon they pass away,
Then comes the long, long day,
Eternity.

"ETERNITY" BY WILL L. THOMPSON

God will fulfill your longing for peace when you spend
eternity with Him. Rest in this truth today as you navigate
your temporary home.

## 28

Therefore, as God's chosen people,
holy and dearly loved,
clothe yourselves with compassion,
kindness, humility, gentleness, and patience.

COLOSSIANS 3:12 NIV

Make it your goal to end the year strong in all of these traits by extending them to the people around you. Give love and watch how your faith grows!

## 29

A lot can change for a person
in a matter of a second,
but just like that it can change again.

CHRISTINA TORRES

Life can do a complete 180 in the blink of an eye. Let your faith serve as an anchor for your soul so that you can withstand the storms.

Beloved, let us love one another,
for love is of God; and everyone who loves
is born of God and knows God.

**1 JOHN 4:7 NKJV**

When you express love, you are shedding God's light on the darkness of the world. Love someone today—bring them the same hope you have!

Give God room to perform miracles.

**ARIAN SIMONE**

Whether this year has been amazing or challenging, whether your faith is stronger than ever or just forming, make room in your heart so God can work miracles through you once more. It's time for another new beginning—of life, hope, and love through God.

# References

Akita, Lailah Gifty. *Pearls of Wisdom: Great Mind*. Goodreads. Accessed March 29, 2019. https://www.goodreads.com/quotes /7417850-every-adversity-brings-new-experiences-and -new-lessons.

Bremer, Carolyn. "Beautiful Bluffton By the Sea, Spring Has Sprung Around Town." *Carolina Morning News*. March 25, 2003.

Buggs, Earlene (@earlenebuggs) 2019. "The funny thing about dreams [...]." Instagram photo, February 16, 2019. https://www .instagram.com/p/Bt8kEbSn3vZ/?utm_source=ig_web_copy_link.

Byler, Linda. *Running Around (And Such)*. Brattleboro, VT: Good Books, 2010.

Caine, Christine. *Undaunted: Daring to Do What God Calls You to Do*. Grand Rapids, MI: Zondervan, 2019.

Chan, Francis, and Danae Yankoski. *Crazy Love: Overwhelmed by a Relentless God*. Colorado Springs, CO: David C. Cook, 2013.

Elliot, Elisabeth. *A Chance to Die: The Life and Legacy of Amy Carmichael*. Grand Rapids, MI: Revell, 2005.

Famous Quotes at BrainyQuote. BrainyQuote. Xplore. Accessed March 29, 2019. https://www.brainyquote.com/.

Giglio, Louie, Francis Chan, Beth Moore, John Piper, Judah Smith, and Christine Caine. *Passion: The Bright Light of Glory*. Nashville, TN: W Publishing Group, an imprint of Thomas Nelson, 2014.

Groeschel, Craig. *Weird: Because Normal Isn't Working.* Grand Rapids, MI: Zondervan, 2011.

Hagee, John (@PastorJohnHagee). 2018. "Stop worrying about what you aren't and start being happy about who you are." Twitter, May 8, 2018. https://twitter.com/PastorJohnHagee /status/993924494057238528.

Hall, Tessa Emily. *Coffee Shop Devos: Daily Devotional Pick-Me-Ups for Teen Girls.* Minneapolis, MN: Bethany House, 2018.

Harrison, Ircel. "Listening to the Spirit in Coaching" April 26, 2018. Accessed March 28, 2019.

Havergal, Frances Ridley. "Another Year Is Dawning." *Baptist Hymnal.* Nashville, TN: LifeWay Worship, 2008.

Henderson, Felecia (@statmentsbyh). 2018. "We have tricked ourselves into incredible smallness, engaging in a fight with our own blindness, not people." Instagram photo, October 31, 2018. https://www.instagram.com/p/BpnB9fVBMmc/?utm_source=ig _web_copy_link.

Herring, Harold. "7 Keys to Spiritual Boldness." HaroldHering.com (blog). Accessed March 29, 2019. https://haroldherring.com/blogs /harolds-blogs/richthoughts/1455-7-keys-to-spiritual-boldness.

Hyles, Jack. "Free Books and Sermons by Dr. Jack Hyles." The Jack Hyles Home Page. Accessed March 29, 2019. http:// www.jackhyles.com/jackhylesquotes.htm.

Hymns Unto God. Accessed March 29, 2019. http://www .hymnsuntogod.org/.

Jakes, Sarah. *Lost and Found: Finding Hope in the Detours of Life.* Bloomington, MN: Bethany House, 2015.

Jakes, T.D. *Reposition Yourself: Living Life Without Limits.* New York, NY: Atria Books, 2008.

Jami, Criss. *Killosophy.* CreateSpace Independent Publishing Platform, 2015.

Jones-Pothier, Kimberly. 2016. "The enemy can't take you out so he's trying to wear you out!" Facebook, December 30, 2016. www.facebook.com/RealTalkKim/posts/the-enemy-cant-take-you -out-so-hes-trying-to-wear-you-out-hes-a-punk-keep-moving /1210170985742419/.

———. 2017. "Don't let the devil shut your mouth, this is the season to declare your deliverance." Facebook, December 21, 2017. www.facebook.com/RealTalkKim/posts/dont-let-the-devil -shut-your-mouth-this-is-the-season-to-declare-your-deliveranc /1543989132360601/.

Keller, Timothy. *Center Church: Doing Balanced, Gospel-Centered Ministry in Your City.* Grand Rapids, MI: Zondervan, 2012.

King, Martin Luther, Jr. "Keep Moving from This Mountain." Speech, Spelman College, Atlanta, May 1, 1960. The Martin Luther King Jr. Research and Education Institute at Stanford University. Accessed March 29, 2019. https://kinginstitute.stanford.edu/king-papers /documents/keep-moving-mountain-address-spelman-college -10-april-1960.

———. "Silent About Things That Matter." Unitarian Universalist Association. June 23, 2016. Accessed March 29, 2019. https://www.uua.org/worship/words/quote/silent-about-things-matter.

Lewis, C.S. *The Problem of Pain.* New York, NY: HarperOne, 2015.

MacArthur, John. "You Are the Only Bible Some Unbelievers Will Ever Read," May 9, 2015, in *Christian Quotes*, produced by Ryan Maher, podcast, MP3 audio, https://radiopublic.com/christian-quotes-encouragement-f-6nEAYW/ep/s1!15020.

Meyer, Joyce. *Battlefield of the Mind: Winning the Battle in Your Mind.* New York, NY: FaithWords, 2011.

Murray, Torres Ilka. 2019. Instagram video, February 11, 2019. https://www.instagram.com/p/BtvahiyBiw_/?utm_source=ig_web_copy_link.

Piper, John. *Desiring God: Meditations of a Christian Hedonist.* Colorado Springs, CO: Multnomah, 2011.

Richmond, Catherine. *Spring for Susannah.* Nashville, TN: Thomas Nelson, 2011.

Shirer, Priscilla. *Fervent: A Woman's Battle Plan for Serious, Specific, and Strategic Prayer.* Nashville, TN: B&H Books, 2015.

Simone, Arian. *Fearless Faith + Hustle: 21 Day Devotional Journey.* Atlanta, GA: Arian Simone Enterprises, 2019.

Sproul, R.C. *A Taste of Heaven: Worship in the Light of Eternity.* Orlando, FL: Reformation Trust Publishing, 2006.

Spurgeon, C.H. *Morning and Evening.* Grand Rapids, MI: Discovery House, 2016.

Stewart, Joyce. *God Is Love: A Spiritual Journey from Fear to Love.* Bloomington, IN: Balboa Press, a Division of Hay House, 2016.

Torres, Carlos (@1torresfamily). 2018. "MOVE-it's what Jesus did!" Instagram photo, March 18, 2018. https://www.instagram.com/p /BgenMV3gH07/?utm_source=ig_web_copy_link.

Torres, Christina (@christinamurray1). 2018. "As my birthday comes to an end I was thinking about a pic to post and I found this one which represents something special to me." Instagram photo, December 29, 2018. https://www.instagram.com/p/Br_41F7F7la /?utm_source=ig_web_copy_link.

Tozer, A.W. *The Pursuit of God: The Human Thirst for the Divine.* Chicago: Moody Publishers, 2015.

Warren, Rick. *The Purpose Driven Life: What on Earth Am I Here For?* 10th ed. Grand Rapids, MI: Zondervan, 2013.

Washer, Paul. *Ten Indictments Against the Modern Church.* Pensacola, FL: Chapel Library, 2012.

White, Carolinne. *The Confessions of St. Augustine.* San Francisco, CA: Ignatius Press: 2007.

Williamson, Marianne. *"A Return to Love: Reflections on the Principles of a Course in Miracles."* San Francisco, CA: HarperOne, 1996.

# Index

# Acknowledgments

I would first like to thank God for everything. This book was God's timing and Godsent and ALL of the glory goes to Him. To my Mother, Andres, Grandma Lily, Juan, Jacob, Jade, Maria, Ilka, Riley, Little Rod, Carlos, Paula, Christian, Jordan Jett, Roman, and the rest of my family, this is for US. We are called for something greater, and the generational curse ends here. Never give up on what God has placed in your heart, because it's bigger than you. To my dearest Romaine, thank you for believing in me and pushing me to follow my heart and God's purpose. You are my true rock, and I am thankful that God gave you to me. To Sydney Vanlandingham, thank you for letting God use you that night during the pool competitions at UTC. That was the pivotal moment that changed the trajectory of my entire life. Because of that moment, I am here today. To my UTC and AIA family, thank you for the memories and lifelong relationships. Lastly, thank you to Callisto Media (Vanessa Putt and Rachel Feldman) for believing in me! All glory to God in the highest!

# About the Author

Jaseña was born and raised in Atlanta, Georgia, where her parents, Christina Torres and Pastor Anthony Murray, founded the Oasis

Family Life Church. As a student at Georgia State University, she studied exercise science and participated in the Ultimate Training Camp for Christian student athletes. It was after that event that she gave her life to Christ and realized her calling for ministry and entrepreneurship.

Jaseña believes in sharing the gospel in a language that people understand and through her artistic abilities. She is currently finishing school, writing, and building her own personal brand and business. In the future, Jaseña hopes that the gifts God has granted her will help break barriers for the gospel of Christ and inspire others to discover their own God-given paths.